DIRTY CASH

Other books in the Virgin True Crime series

DIRTY CASH

Organised Crime in the 21st Century

David Southwell

First published in Great Britain in 2002 by

Virgin Books Ltd
Thames Wharf Studios
Rainville Road
London W6 9HA

A catalogue record for this book is available from the British Library

ISBN 0 7535 0702 1

Typeset by TW Typesetting, Plymouth, Devon.
Printed and bound in Great Britain by
Mackays of Chatham PLC

CONTENTS

INTRODUCTION

Many people do not realise that organised crime is a business much like any legitimate operation. Its methods are frequently evil, its ruthlessness greater than that of most corporations, and the activities it deals in are despicable and predatory but, that aside, there's not a huge difference between the ways in which the criminal world and legitimate industry operate. Technological advances have given us access to information and communication systems on a scale we could not have anticipated even as recently as the mid 1990s. Business has been quick to respond; corporations have globalised, entered into strategic alliances, streamlined staffing, made private agreements, and become leaner, harder and sharper. So has organised crime.

The public tends to view organised crime with a certain amount of romantic nostalgia. But the image of the ruthless but sympathetic boss running a patch of the city with the help of his pals, preying mostly on other criminals and keeping the public out of it is an illusion – a folk memory of the likes of Robin Hood and Dick Turpin (loveable rogues who are out to rob the rich in the name of justice) or 'rough-diamond' East End lads and stern Italian wiseguys, as portrayed on celluloid by Bob Hoskins or Robert de Niro. Either way, these images are a myth that helps criminal interests to continue. The small gangs of villains keeping themselves to themselves and fiercely resisting all invaders are gone, in the same way that the family-run butcher and the friendly corner shop giving personal customer service are gone.

The terrifying truth is that modern transnational criminal organisations (TCOs) are adaptable, sophisticated, extremely opportunistic and fully involved with a huge range of illegal (and legal) activities. Today's master criminals are not gun-waving psychotics. They are accountants and lawyers and directors, sitting behind expensive desks in tasteful penthouse offices co-ordinating their many and various 'business' interests. They have meetings with other criminal organisations, plan global strategies, make business agreements, and trade expertise with one another. They operate across the world, taking advantage of loopholes and havens wherever available, passing dirty money through legitimate businesses in order to launder it clean. They apply their well-practised criminal skills as part of their legal day-to-day business operations. Like any other businessmen, when their interests are threatened they take action to defend them – but, unlike most other businesses, they will not hesitate to use violence, torture, bribery or murder to get a competitive advantage.

The new criminal order has interests everywhere. Some of their low-level activities, such as street crime, robbery, car theft and drug dealing, have unfortunately become commonplace, blighting our cities and, increasingly, even rural areas across Europe and America. Other activities are more covert – everything from environmental crime and smuggling migrants to trading in knock-off perfume, pirate software and bootleg cigarettes. Sounds harmless enough, until you realise that the bloke down the pub your mate gets cheap DVDs from is part of the same vast network that murders peace campaigners and enslaves children. It's a sobering thought.

Getting in the way can be fatal. Russian media commentators were shocked by the surprising number of deaths – almost fifty – amongst campaigners opposing a 1998 corporate merger that placed forty per cent of

Russian aluminium production in the hands of one company. It is now believed that the company is affiliated to a Russian-based TCO, and that the criminals were determined to make sure that the merger went through, by any means necessary.

As those working outside society's laws become ever more experienced at exploiting the new global nature of trade and finance and recent developments in technology, the threat from organised crime is burgeoning. Creative, sophisticated criminals are always trying to keep one step ahead of government intelligence services; they work hard to discover new methods and opportunities for smuggling drugs and other contraband, or carrying out huge financial crimes, frauds and money-laundering operations. The new opportunities seem endless. As if that were not enough, previously legitimate businesses are being drawn into criminal economic practice just so that they can compete with organised crime. It is rumoured that some major cigarette manufacturers have been smuggling their products across national borders – with or without criminal assistance.

The threat associated with organised criminal activity falls into three fairly distinct categories. Firstly there is the threat to individuals and the security and welfare of the law-abiding public. The next level involves the dangers faced by businesses and institutions, such as fraud, theft, corruption, piracy, intellectual property theft and loss through being undercut. This damages competitiveness, increases instability in the business world, and costs a lot of people their jobs every year. The final level of threat is to global security, safety and stability, through environmental crime, the trafficking of arms and weapons of mass destruction, and the corruption of political and legal systems. This causes untold misery and suffering around the world.

Drug smuggling and arms trafficking are generally considered to be the most corrosive of organised criminal activities in terms of the number of lives they affect, but environmental crime, slavery and illegal immigration are also high up the list. Money-laundering, however, is the crime considered most *economically* important to the TCOs: it is absolutely vital to make cash available for use without leaving a trail back to the criminal.

One further catastrophic side effect of international criminal activity has been the expansion of terrorist activities. TCOs have taken advantage of a number of international financial and political changes and, in many cases, they may have helped to bring them about. Restrictive repression of alcohol, drugs or gambling is good for criminal business, for instance; similarly, there are always countries where changes in financial regulations help to create new tax havens and money-laundering possibilities. The same networks, loopholes, computer scams and pathways that allow TCOs to flourish are also now being used by terrorist organisations. In addition to increasing the general scope and reach of the terrorist groups' activities, some criminal outfits also become international criminal organisations in their own right to fund political murders, and some enlist already-established criminal groups to help them get hold of better weaponry and other equipment. The criminal organisations will sell to *anyone* who has the money.

Organised crime is a menace, exploiting the world's most vulnerable people and making billions of dollars out of their misery. The desperate situation of many of those at the mercy of the tyranny of these gangs and their despicable trade should be remembered when we are tempted to look at criminals with rose-tinted glasses.

Dirty Cash will look at the nuts and bolts of the TCOs, their businesses and how they operate. The facts make chilling reading.

1. THE NEW CRIMINAL ORDER AND THEIR BUSINESSES

DRUG SMUGGLING

The illicit drugs trade remains one of the biggest threats to the stability and welfare of society across the western world. It is not only the horrendous cost in terms of immediate human suffering that is so worrying (drug addiction is a major contributor to a number of endemic health problems including HIV/AIDS, hepatitis, pneumonia, injury and malnourishment), but the knock-on effects are proving to be equally devastating. Hardened drug use feeds street crime, sexual exploitation and violence, and also devastates family and neighbourhood bonds. It can be the source of child abuse and terrible parenting of the kind that locks the children of drug-addicted parents into a life-long spiral of poverty, crime and despair.

US Government reports estimate that one person in fifteen over the age of 12 is an active drug user – including over three million regular hardcore abusers of cocaine or its refined form, crack, and almost a million regular users of heroin. The American Office of National Drug Control Policy estimates that drug use killed over 52,000 people and cost US society $110 billion in 1995, and, during 1998, accounted for a third of all new AIDS cases in men, and almost half of all new AIDS cases in women.

These levels of drug consumption are thought to be consistent across western society, but these statistics on their own still do not reflect the social damage caused by drug abuse and the crime associated with it. Regular hardened drug use is strongly linked with antisocial behaviour patterns, disrespect for the law and for social institutions, and high levels of street crime and violence – caused both by addicts needing to obtain the money to feed their habits, and by dealers fighting over territory, customer bases and distribution. Over two thirds of all adult males arrested in the USA on criminal charges in 1998 tested positive for at least one drug – and some sixty per cent of the prison population is there as a result of drug-related crime. Much the same is true across northern Europe.

Organisations that deal in international drug smuggling build up vast networks of suppliers, and the bogus companies that act as fronts, provide ways to make smuggling easier and give opportunities to launder the profits. As the trade has evolved in the last ten years, it has grown considerably with an increasing number of organisations involved in production, trafficking and distribution. Even the TCOs that used to concentrate on traditional activities such as fraud, racketeering and street crime have become involved in trafficking. While not actually producing drugs themselves, Russian, Chinese, Albanian and Italian criminal organisations are involved in drug distribution and smuggling. Many groups are putting aside old hostilities and ethnic biases and are forming partnerships with a diversity of groups so as to make the purchase, smuggling and dealing of illegal drugs more efficient. Even organisations that traditionally avoided drugs, such as rebel movements, freedom fighters, terror organisations and extremist groups – from the IRA to the Ku Klux Klan – have turned to the narcotics trade to help raise funds.

Increasingly open borders and new developments in communications have given international drugs traffickers the opportunity to become ever more sophisticated and flexible. They are quick to compensate for law enforcement efforts by finding new ways of hiding smuggled drugs, trying unexpected shipping routes, spreading loads among multiple couriers, and discovering new ways of laundering the profits. In many of the production centres, particularly for cocaine and heroin, drugs organisations have gained a significant amount of political power through extortion, intimidation, bribery and blackmail. They will do whatever is required to protect their interests, including taking violent action against international law enforcement agents, journalists and other researchers who are seen to be getting in the way.

The drugs trade has greatly destabilised a number of major producing countries, reducing living standards, causing significant amounts of domestic drug addiction, weakening economies and spreading AIDS amongst large numbers of the population. These problems cause tensions that are felt in the entire region surrounding the producer nation, and fuel the increasing risk of social instability and war. In Colombia, for example, the fight against paramilitary groups funded by cocaine traffic has cost as much as six per cent of the country's gross domestic product (GDP) and has taken the lives of a million people under the age of 18. The troubled central Asian republics are also crippled by drugs-related problems. According to some estimates, up to thirty per cent of Tajikistan's GDP is attributable to the trade in hashish, opium and heroin, while Uzbekistan and Kazakhstan have around 200,000 heroin addicts each. Russia now has two million cases of HIV, the 'leakage' of heroin from Afghanistan is creating a generation of Pakistani and Iranian addicts and, in Myanmar (Burma), there are thought to be nearly half a million HIV-positive junkies.

Drugs production is an industry that spans the globe. Cocaine is produced in South America, chiefly in Colombia, Bolivia and Peru. It is generally refined into crack in the local area of its destination. Most of the world's heroin is manufactured in Asia, primarily in the 'Golden Crescent' of Afghanistan and Pakistan, and the 'Golden Triangle' of Thailand, Burma and Laos. Colombia and Mexico also provide heroin for the US market. Surprisingly, substantial quantities of methamphetamines come from the same regions as heroin and follow similar distribution lines, although the majority of this drug is manufactured in the US and Mexico. Ecstasy (MDMA) mostly originates in Europe, and is produced in the Netherlands and Poland. It is shipped through Amsterdam, Brussels, Frankfurt and Paris, entering other European countries directly, and finding its way to the Americas via Surinam, Curacao and the Dominican Republic.

Cannabis is produced in quantity in a number of regions across the world, including Morocco, Afghanistan, Thailand, Mexico, Canada, Jamaica, Cambodia and Lebanon. It remains the most commonly used drug by a long way, and is also the most readily available. While most abusers of hard drugs start off with cannabis, the reverse does not hold true; most cannabis users do not move to hard drugs. Drugs think-tanks suggest that it is the criminalisation of cannabis that pushes some of its users to harder drugs, rather than the drug itself, and police in many regions of the UK are now softening their stance on cannabis, although this policy is still in the early stages of experimentation.

However paradoxical it may seem, the legalisation of any illegal drug is extremely bad news for the criminal organisations. The loudest voice in favour of keeping softer drugs illegal has always belonged to organised crime. The reasons are simple: if a substance is banned, demand does not go away, but the only suppliers remain the criminals. However harmless smoking a joint once in a while may be, while cannabis remains illegal it has to be obtained from a dealer. That dealer has to obtain it from a distributor, who will in turn be linked back, eventually, to a major criminal organisation. The TCOs set the price, control the market, decide the quality, and reap the immense profits. Legalising and licensing soft drugs such as cannabis – thought by many to be less harmful medically than tobacco and alcohol – would immediately transfer a huge chunk of profit from the criminal organisations to the government.

In addition, legal production would allow standards and safety checks to be put in place. Most criminally sold drugs are mixed with cheaper chemicals and other agents to increase profit margins – everything from talcum powder to bleach to horse tranquillisers. These 'fillers' are often a lot more harmful than the drug itself, sometimes even lethal. The criminal organisations don't mind a certain rate of death amongst users; when one addict falls, another will step up to take his place.

However, in the UK, the decriminalisation of even the softest drugs is controversial generally and a political hot potato. Certain sectors of the media are quick to react whenever the issue is debated in the House of Commons. Politicians and lobbyists further stir up extremist opinion and make reasoned debate difficult. Just like alcohol prohibition in the 1920s, the present-day 'war on drugs' usually only serves to strengthen criminal interests, while making politicians popular with a manipulated population.

ILLEGAL IMMIGRATION AND SLAVERY

Groups that engage in smuggling 'human cargo' manage the import of foreign nationals into a target country, their route taking them from poor or overcrowded countries to the prosperous western world. The transport process is often cramped and dangerous, as the fifty-eight dead Chinese immigrants found in the back of a truck stopped in Dover in June 2000 so tragically indicated.

The past two decades have seen Europe undergo significant upheavals and changes: the collapse of Communism in the east, the fall of the Berlin Wall, and war in the Balkan states; these factors have contributed to thousands of people being on the move. Migrants from Third World countries can now take different routes to reach western Europe than those which they used 20 or 30 years ago. The end of Communism has meant that people have been able to transit through the countries of the former Soviet Union and eastern Europe far more easily than in the past.

Once they arrive in the target country, illegal immigrants generally vanish into their particular ethnic communities, where they find work and accommodation. The majority of illegal immigrants come to the First World for economic reasons, desperate to escape crushing poverty with no prospect of improvement. A few, however, are criminals, terrorists and extremists.

The US Immigration and Naturalization Service estimates that as much as two per cent of the entire population of North America are illegal, undocumented immigrants. The problem may not be as severe in Britain and the other European countries – Mexicans make up just over half of all illegal US immigrants – but it is on a similar scale. Whilst it is easy to understand why people would want to get away from hopeless situations, the presence of illegal immigrants does add a degree of strain to available social resources and a country's economy. It contributes to crime, and stirs increasing anger and unhappiness in the domestic population. On top of this, the poor wages and working conditions that illegal immigrants are prepared to tolerate have a knock-on effect, driving down pay and conditions for legal and indigenous workers.

There is also no doubt that there are links between illegal immigrant smuggling, drug trafficking and terrorist, extremist and criminal organisations. Some illegal immigrants are used as 'mules', smuggling both themselves and drugs shipments. Others are smuggled into a country specifically to work on dangerous criminal operations; Russian, Nigerian and Chinese criminal groups are all known to import people for high-risk activities. The lack of any official information on the illegal immigrant makes it harder for law enforcement to investigate the criminals or their links to larger organisations.

The wholesale illegal importation of people also raises serious human rights issues. The bulk of illegal immigrants come to the west willingly, looking for a better chance to make money, and a higher standard of living. They will have to pay the criminal organisations a lot of money for the opportunity, sometimes saving up for years. Many are abused – both en route and when they reach their destination. Some die during the journey, either as a result of the poor conditions that they are shipped in or because of the way their handlers treat them. If official forces spot the smugglers, immigrants may be left to die without food or water in deserted places, or tossed overboard. The few such incidents that have been discovered and reported make grim reading. In 2001 fourteen Mexican immigrants died after being abandoned by their smugglers in the middle of the Arizona desert. In 1998 dozens of Sri Lankans died locked in an airless lorry container on the Austrian border, while in the early 1990s a group of Iraqis were robbed by their handlers and left to drown in the Aegean.

If the immigrants arrive safely, conditions are poor. Most work in hard manual jobs for a pittance. They may still owe a lot of money to the people who smuggled them, and may have to work for years to pay the criminals off. Because they have no legal status, they have little protection from the forces of law and order. They may even be forced into criminal activity or *de facto* slavery to pay off their debts.

Even more disturbingly, many criminal organisations actually deal in slaves, especially women and children. Most of these victims will end up being used for sexual exploitation or forced labour – and the problem is increasing. The people stuck in these situations are routinely abused and exploited, and may be forced to work as prostitutes, sex slaves, sweatshop machine operators, servants and crop-pickers. They live in a continual atmosphere of violence, cruelty, abuse and rape. US Government figures estimate that 700,000 enslaved women and children are moved across international borders each year, and that the sex industry worldwide earns at least $4 billion each year from slavery. There are a number of non-governmental organisations across the world that put both figures considerably higher. Some of the victims are illegal migrants who are simply never given their freedom, while many others each year are conned, kidnapped, or sold by desperate families. Victims are often forcibly addicted to hard drugs to keep them compliant. Few slavery victims are ever recovered, and convictions are rare.

The organisations frequently target women in countries where prospects are grim, particularly where criminal interests are dominant, and women traditionally have subordinate roles. The problem is especially bad in South America, South East Asia and the former Soviet Union. Victims are often fooled into leaving the country by fake offers of a better job abroad as a model, dancer, maid or waitress. Their friends and family, thinking they are emigrating with a *bona fide* group, cause no problems. Others, particularly children, may just be quietly sold – often at gunpoint – to the slavers. Once the victims are en route, they may be forced into drug addiction, tortured or terrorised with threats to family and friends in order to secure compliance. They are then sold into slavery. Over 200,000 women and children from South East Asia were enslaved in 1997, almost half of them under the age of 18. Most were sold to buyers in other countries within the region, such as Japan, Australia, Hong Kong and Singapore, although the US Government estimates that 30,000 were sold to clients inside the USA. Just under 200,000 were enslaved in the former Soviet countries and Eastern Europe in the same year, most ending up in Germany, Italy and Holland.

The groups that smuggle immigrants and slaves are highly practised at moving people across national borders. Illegal immigrant operations are usually based around loose networks of agents in a variety of locations, forming a chain of local operators rather than a rigidly structured top-controlled gang. One set of agents obtains the people for transportation, another group provides false identification and documents, and various other operators along the transport route will move the group along on each stage of the operation. This allows the groups to vary their routes quickly and effectively, and to continue business without missing a beat if one agent in the chain is arrested or compromised. The people being transported will be handed from smuggler to smuggler many times, making it very difficult to disrupt the network. Most of the people smuggled into Europe come in either from Russia and Asia through the eastern European countries – where border controls are patchy at best – or from Africa via Mediterranean coastal areas, particularly Italy and Spain. Once within the EU, the Scheveningen Agreement on internal border relaxation makes it easy to relocate the people. Getting into the UK is a bit trickier, but not much so, as the continual problems with Channel Tunnel security so clearly demonstrate. In the USA, they are brought over the Mexican border. Illegal immigrants usually refuse to admit their original home country when caught, so have to be deported back to the country they just entered from; most barely pause before continuing on their journey.

Although traditionally the gangs involved in human slavery are small, the major criminal organisations are increasingly coming to dominate, as it is such a profitable business. The slavers often use legitimate-seeming companies as a cover for their operations – job agencies, marriage bureaux, travel agencies or entertainment troupes. Legitimate documentation is usually obtained, with the victim vanishing after arrival, but they will resort to faked documents and bribery when necessary. The victims are usually moved by commercial airlines, appearing as tourists. They may change flights a number of times, however, and the group will change routes frequently. The problem is complicated because, in the source country, the victim may well be operating of his or her own free will – and local police avoid getting involved, reasoning that any illegal coercion will take place outside their jurisdiction. In April 1997, four senior Bulgarian officials, two of whom worked in law enforcement, were simply sacked – but faced no further charges – when they were found to be linked to an organised crime group procuring female slaves for prostitution. Meanwhile, the problem continues to escalate.

ENVIRONMENTAL CRIME

While it may seem petty at first glance when compared to drug running and slavery, environmental crime is one of the most profitable and dangerous new sectors of transnational criminal business, and it has the potential to have extremely serious consequences for all of us. As international environmental awareness has evolved over the last fifteen years, the number of conventions, laws, treaties and regulations aimed at controlling hazards to both health and nature have increased. Toxic wastes and pollutants need to be controlled properly, limited resources have to be carefully managed, and endangered species require protection. Waste disposal costs, particularly for toxic waste, have soared, and restricted natural resources have gained greatly in value. High costs means that the criminal organisations can make a lot of money – up to $30 billion annually – and several have moved in to take advantage, particularly those from Russia, China, Italy and Japan.

The costs associated with making hazardous chemicals, toxic waste and other dangerous pollutants safe for disposal are immense. Criminal organisations can accrue vast amounts of money by legally taking on the contracts to dispose of the toxic materials, and then mixing them in with recyclables, domestic waste and scrap metals and dumping them without any treatment or preparation. Lax legislation and limited penalties in various

European, African and Asian countries make them particularly tempting targets for dumping toxic wastes, particularly where 'trash for cash' schemes offer dumps for safe international waste in return for nominal fees. Standard criminal leverage helps make sure that the organisation front companies that get the contracts, and that no one asks too many questions at the other end.

Italian organisations are particularly successful in this field as they are well established in the country's waste disposal sector. Italian authorities estimate that half of the country's 80 million tons of waste is illegally dumped in unsafe locations. They claim that the majority of Italian waste disposal companies are fronts for Mafia and related organisations. In 1997, authorities estimate that the 53 different crime groups trafficking toxic waste dumped 11 million tons of hazardous materials into the Mediterranean sea, or into rivers which will feed into it, with the remaining missing materials being shipped to Eastern Europe, Albania and West Africa.

Radioactive waste material from France, Austria, Germany and several eastern European countries is known to make its way routinely into the Mediterranean and Adriatic seas courtesy of Italian criminal gangs. Given that these areas are prime tourist districts and the source of a lot of European fish production, there is plenty of cause for concern. The damage that waste-related crime causes to human health, natural bio-systems and the planet's environment may not become apparent for several years, but it will be significant. These wastes inevitably enter the human food chain and get fed to all of us worldwide. Their legacy will include cancers, birth defects and diseases on top of the more obvious extinction of wildlife and habitat destruction.

* * *

Stolen, illegally harvested, or otherwise banned natural resources also provide significant revenue for organised crime – up to $8 billion a year. Criminal organisations from all around the globe are involved in illegally cutting down and selling restricted forest timber. Criminal logging activity has led to a substantial decline in forested areas worldwide, not only destroying all manner of irreplaceable natural habitats but also hastening global warming. Fish stocks are similarly being destroyed beyond recovery – Russian and Chinese organisations make a lot of money from illegal fishing. Not only does this greatly harm fish populations – which are already starting to vanish completely in several areas – but it also damages local fishing industries and eats into government revenues. Much of this illegally caught fish is sold to Japan. Japanese figures show that in 1997 the country imported over $1 billion of fish from Russia; this is six times as much as Russian figures say was exported.

Endangered animals – whole or in chunks – also sell for high prices across the Far East. This trade is said to be worth up to $10 billion a year. Elephants, whales, turtles, tigers, rhinos and exotic birds and reptiles are the most commonly poached species. Poaching operations are not small, local businesses undertaken by desperate locals; they are slick, well-organised military-style operations co-ordinated by international criminal organisations, particularly from China and other Asian countries.

ARMS SMUGGLING

The illegal sale of armaments is a serious threat to us all. The end markets for illegal arms tend to include rogue states, terrorist organisations, freedom fighters, countries placed under sanctions or embargoes, and major criminal organisations. Since the end of the Cold War with its attendant scaling down of military operations in many countries, considerable amounts of hardware have become available on the black market. Political and economic disintegration in Russia and the Warsaw Pact countries has further added to this illicit stockpile, making even complete fighter planes and helicopters available. The most commonly smuggled armaments include spare parts for complicated or large-scale weaponry, assault rifles, rocket-launchers and single-operator missiles, explosives, and a vast array of ammunition. Large-scale military offence and defence systems are also sold, although not as frequently. Sales to sanctioned countries alone are estimated to be worth hundreds of millions of dollars annually.

The majority of illegal weapons sales are hidden behind a façade of legitimate exports. False papers are generally used to hide the recipient or the fact that the goods being shipped are weapons. Illegal arms have been smuggled into Afghanistan and the former Yugo-slavian republics under the guise of humanitarian aid. Sometimes the supplier's identity is also faked. This allows for relatively regular shipping and fund transfer procedures – fairly important when a deal may involve hundreds of tons of equipment, and be worth tens of millions of dollars. This procedure is referred to as 'grey-market' smuggling. By contrast, black-market arms are simply hidden, using the same sorts of procedures as drugs shipments. There is no attempt to provide even semi-accurate documentation. While this does increase deniability and avoid leaving a paper trail, it gets harder to carry out as the size of the shipment increases. Sneaking six jet fighters over a border is a lot harder than bringing over three kilos of C4 explosive. Because of their proximity to the violence and anarchy in the Balkan states – particularly the former Yugoslavia – organisations in Russia and Italy have become particularly active in this field.

CONTRABAND

Non-drug contraband smuggling is defined as the illegal export and/or import of legitimate goods – everything from spirits and tobacco through to cars and manufactured items. It can be extremely profitable when local taxes and tariffs are high or the goods are expensive, and the legal penalties associated with it are generally much lighter than those associated with smuggling drugs, weapons or gems. Criminal organisations from all over the globe use contraband to bolster profits. By cutting out tax payments and selling at a considerably lower price than standard market value, these organisations do governments and domestic businesses out of a substantial chunk of revenue. They distort the marketplace, and may be seriously sub-standard – spoiled or pesticide-laden food, adulterated or ineffective pharmaceuticals. If the goods were originally stolen, then there is the added benefit of greater safety in disposing of the merchandise. The greater the amount of cross-border commercial trade, the less chance there is of smuggling being detected, so the largest smuggling routes are the same as the largest conventional trade routes.

The majority of smuggled contraband is physically hidden when crossing a border, or is disguised through faked documentation. False invoices, inaccurate goods valuations and complex transfer price agreements are all used to muddy the waters. In addition, over-valuation of a shipment is a common way of providing an apparently legitimate trail for funds to be hidden in, allowing them to be laundered. Under-valuation, on the other hand, helps the smuggler to avoid proper taxation. In some cases, the goods are legitimately exported, and then 'stolen' in transit by prior arrangement through fake hijackings or staged accidents.

The general public is frequently enthusiastic about contraband, particularly when the savings are good. Cigarettes, alcohol and cars are commonly smuggled because government duties tend to be a large percentage of the end price. Public revenue losses can be huge. The EU estimates that smuggled cigarettes cost its member states almost $4 billion in lost tax revenue in 1999. China and Russia have some of the highest import tariffs on goods designated 'luxuries', so they are favoured destinations for smuggled shipments. In Colombia, many drugs cartels combine money laundering with smuggling by purchasing cigarettes with the proceeds from drugs sales, and then smuggling them back into the country for sale on the black market.

Meanwhile, the USA remains a vitally important destination for smuggled contraband of all kinds. According to US Customs, more than one and a quarter million people enter the USA every day, with almost half a million vehicles, including slightly under fifty thousand trucks, lorries and containers. US Customs is only able to inspect three per cent of all goods entering the country – and that number is expected to drop to one per cent by the end of the year 2007. That offers an excellent chance of getting a shipment into the country – the loss of one shipment in thirty is trivial if each consignment is fairly small. Interestingly, the USA has a particular appetite for smuggled CFCs. The high rate of US taxation on CFC use – designed to help protect the environment by regulating use of ozone-destroying gases – makes them a profitable contraband item. The mark-up on black market CFCs is often as much as

1000 per cent, and tens of thousands of tons are smuggled into the country every year.

Unlike many organised criminal activities, contraband trade is two-way. Significant amounts of contraband are smuggled out of western countries and into the developing world. Restricted commodities associated with military purposes are always popular, along with the machinery required to produce weapons. Stolen luxury items are also a popular smuggled export. For instance, the USA is a source of a substantial quantity of contraband cars, cigarettes and alcohol. It is also a prime source for illegal handguns, because of their common availability compared to most other countries.

The market for stolen cars is huge, mostly flowing from the west to China and Russia. In the USA, Russian and Asian TCOs use street gangs to obtain cars, then pass them to Mexican organisations to smuggle them out of the country, before they are exported semi-legitimately to their end destinations, usually in large sea containers. The stolen cars may further be used to hide drugs, small arms, or other additional contraband. Vehicle security experts alter car identification details, including engine block details, to help obscure any possible trail. The entire process is extremely professional at all levels. EU law enforcement agencies reckon that cars worth $5 billion are stolen and exported out of Europe every year. In America, the FBI estimate that one and a half million cars are stolen each year in the USA, and that around $4 billion worth are smuggled out of the country. Less than one in a hundred cars stolen for contraband is ever recovered.

MONEY LAUNDERING

Few things arouse official suspicion as quickly as large sums of unexplained money. The banking system has checks in place to make sure that transfers and proceeds are logged, and there are statutory requirements to inform law enforcement agencies when cash sums in excess of certain thresholds are deposited. If money seems to be coming out of nowhere, it is very quickly noticed and investigated. The only legitimate way to regularly generate financial income is by conducting legal business, so if you have a regular income that is not obviously linked to standard business activity, it will generate a lot of attention. Criminal proceeds need to be seen to be coming from somewhere in order to avoid making the police and tax authorities suspicious, and money laundering provides that phoney legitimacy.

There are other benefits, of course. By moving the money through a maze of different businesses and countries, criminal organisations make it effectively impossible for law enforcement agencies to identify its source. That helps protect the organisation and its contacts, effectively hiding internal links and structures. It also makes the money far harder to confiscate if legal action is taken. The profits generated by criminal activity can be seized by government agents – it goes into government coffers, of course, rather than back to the end victims – but if the money has been properly laundered there is no way of identifying it as criminal proceeds, and it is untouchable.

Once money has been laundered – effectively 'washed clean' of the dirty stains of crime – it is free for use in any capacity. Once organisation members are paid for the legitimate work that they seem to do, remaining funds are used to finance further criminal activity. Laundered money may be passed through another set of false businesses and accounts before being used in this way, so as to make doubly sure that it cannot be traced back to the criminals involved.

For obvious reasons, it is almost impossible to assess accurately the amount of money that gets laundered. If it were possible to identify laundered funds enough to count them, they could also be backtracked, linked to criminal activity, used to prove culpability, and confiscated. Internationally, intelligence agencies, legal bodies and financial analysts all agree that a huge amount is laundered every year, and that this is growing steadily. Because of the uncertainties involved, no agency has managed to provide a solid answer as to how much dirty money is laundered, but there have been a number of informed guesses. One of the International Monetary Fund's former managing directors has suggested that as much as five per cent of all commercial activity worldwide is actually laundered criminal funds – a staggering $2 *trillion* annually.

As well as enabling criminal organisations to continue their activities, money laundering has a number of adverse effects in its own right. On a general economic level, it increases the unpredictability of the currency exchange markets, and distorts interest rates and market predictions. This instability causes problems for the people setting economic policy, and can weaken pension and savings returns, and inflate tax. On a more immediate scale, money laundering can provide problems for governments trying to collect tax, and increases the cost of policing the banking and financial sectors, and business in general. All of these issues further add to the cost of the tax that we all have to pay.

In weaker countries – which may have a low GDP, be financially naïve compared to the west, or be in the process of modernising – the transfer and storage of large amounts of dirty cash can seriously undermine the economy and the government. Criminal business fronts for laundering funds frequently out-compete or terrorise their honest rivals, thus frightening off investors and making them wary of the entire sector. Some of the newer, more complicated modern frauds that require large sums of free cash may not be familiar to finance professionals in the country. In Albania in the mid 1990s, a complex pyramid fraud scheme masterminded by Italian crime groups stole the savings of almost half the population shortly after the economy was deregulated. The money was not recoverable, as the fraud had not been legislated against.

In countries that are actively trying to bring their banking sector in line with modern western standards, criminal financial interests can be an immense problem. Corrupt officials and politicians will use every possible resource and excuse to impede progress, weaken legislation, confuse issues and generally stand in the way of reform. To make matters worse, modern banking relies heavily on accurate and closely followed risk assessment in order to remain stable and profitable. TCO-run banks do not have any interest in actuarially sound banking. They finance illegal ventures, risky but strategically important businesses, provide dubious loans to associated mobsters, and harass rivals. They are run as a tool and weapon of the criminal organisation, which makes them lousy financial institutions. Their weakness makes the entire sector shakier. Any bank collapsing is always bad news for a country's financial and political stability, and it is worse when the collapse is linked to organised crime.

There are a lot of different ways to launder money effectively, and all the TCOs have large, sophisticated worldwide networks covering all of the possible methods. These allow the huge amounts of money that they generate to be filtered down through a bewildering array of different channels, spreading the risks of detection and further protecting their own identities. One of the most popular ways of laundering money is to run a legitimate business – particularly one that deals primarily in cash – and slip dirty money into the daily takings. Casinos, restaurants, hotels and travel agencies are all very popular, because they see a lot of cash-flow, and their day-to-day sales are very difficult to verify from stock. These businesses are usually profitable in their own right, too, further adding to income. As well as being a good way to hide illegal funds, they also give individual criminals a convincing source for their personal incomes.

The banking sector provides a number of convenient ways of laundering proceeds. The financial markets – stocks, securities, currency exchanges – deal in huge sums on a minute-by-minute basis, and the complex web of transactions leaping from currency to currency makes it very hard to keep track of individual sums. The largest world markets, such as the FTSE, Dow Jones, Nikkei and Han Seng, are so vast that, despite a tight regulation and law enforcement, they remain popular and common ways of purifying finances. Many TCOs actually acquire ownership of legitimate banks in order to increase their security on the stock markets, while others place agents within major banks as legitimate employees. Banks that operate strict secrecy policies – Swiss banks, for example – are a huge boon for money laundering operations, as cash can be moved in and out without being easily identifiable.

Organised gambling is another good way of cleaning profits. All games of chance have a predictable rate of return in the long run. For many forms of gambling, the rate of loss overall is not as high as might be expected. That is particularly true when the results can be fixed – horse racing, for example. Bookies and casinos deal in huge sums of cash daily, both in and out, so large sums do not raise any suspicion. Even if the organisation does not own a particular gambling operation, the loss associated with careful betting is considerably less than government tax would be, and the money that comes out the other end is completely clean. When the organisation both runs the bookies and fixes the races – often the case – the laundering process itself becomes extremely profitable.

Some money launderers have been known to use informal banking systems, such as the Hawala system in the Arab world and the *fei qian* ('flying money') system in China, to transfer funds around the world. Because these methods are organised on a basis of personal relationships – members of the same clan, village or family agreeing to make and receive payments in different places – they leave almost no paper trail. But there are also a few large-scale financial institutions that are not linked to the international banking network, and are relatively lightly regulated.

Colombia has developed its own method of money laundering – the black market peso exchange. Drugs money banked in the US is sold wholesale to brokers, who pay for the dollars with appropriately valued Colombian accounts holding pesos. The brokers then sell the dollars cheaply to Colombian businessmen and entrepreneurs visiting the US, in return for pesos deposited at home in Colombia. The purchasers typically use the dollars they buy to obtain US goods and services, which are then exported back home. What began as drugs money effectively ends up as cheaply sold foreign exchange. US agencies estimate that the black peso exchange launders up to $5 billion each year.

There are a number of factors that help to determine how suitable a country is as a haven for money laundering. These include laws protecting banks' rights to secrecy, corruption within financial institutions, poor or naïve legislation, ineffective legal enforcement of existing laws, and lax regulatory control over the banking sector. Offshore tax havens are particularly useful. Liechtenstein, the Cayman Islands, Israel and Lebanon are all popular destinations. They typically provide a high degree of tax and company secrecy, combined with low rates of tax, and cheap, easy-to-form companies. These are powerful incentives to criminal organisations. Some of the new wave of offshore tax havens, such as the ones emerging in the South Pacific, are also very lightly regulated.

Russia and the former Soviet bloc countries are making the change to free-market economies, and criminal organisations have used the opportunity offered by privatisations and developing sectors to get a significant foothold within the banking sector. Law enforcement is sporadic at best, and loose regulation combined with a general absence of money laundering checks make the area very useful. The criminal community has a lot of real power in many parts of Russia, making it very difficult to control illegal financial activity. Latin America is also very useful. Bank secrecy is commonly protected, staff have little or no training, laws are sloppy, and corruption is endemic. Many South American countries also only legislate against the laundering of drugs proceeds, leaving it legal to launder other criminal profits.

INTELLECTUAL PROPERTY THEFT
Intellectual Property (usually called IP) is a broad, catch-all term for a range of intangible assets, such as logos, patents, concepts, trademarks and copyrights, trade secrets, specific images and text,

fictional characters and settings, and general look and feel. IP crime generally involves violating patents, stealing trade secrets, or infringing copyright and trademarks – which covers the production of everything from pirate software to fake perfume. Counterfeit and pirate products damage the IP-producing businesses, undermining their performance and slashing their income. Whilst the Internet is particularly notorious as a source of pirate music, software and photos, the range of options for digital scanning has made it much easier to copy and distribute everything from logos to confidential research.

IP crime is a particular problem for western countries because of the huge number of companies whose business is intellectual property – and the majority of counterfeit goods are facsimiles of western items. The USA in particular is the world's largest creator and exporter of intellectual properties – in the forms of computer software products, audio and music recordings, book publishing, television and movies. In 1996, these 'copyright industry' products made up almost four per cent of the US GDP, worth some $270 billion – and what is more, they were America's main export.

It is therefore significant that bootleg products are coming to affect sales of legal goods more and more. Western companies are losing a lot of money through sales that go to illegally manufactured and distributed products. While some counterfeit material is sold domestically, the majority is sold outside the West, in open competition with genuine articles. Sometimes the fake products are so prevalent in a country that the real product owners are unable to distribute their own goods.

Stolen trade secrets also represent a significant loss of market share and profitability for western businesses. Foreign companies and even some governments are keen to get hold of sensitive trade information. Proprietary information such as strategic planning, confidential bids, advanced production systems and research and development can be worth hundreds of millions in lost contracts. By reducing the competitiveness of western firms in the global market, foreign competitors seek to find ways to undercut or disadvantage western companies. American estimates suggest that in 2000, industrial espionage alone cost US industry as much as $45 billion. But the overall effect is greater than just lost sales. Figures based on activity in 1998 suggest that the total annual loss to the US economy in terms of tax, lost jobs and diverted sales is more than $200 billion. It is thought that IP violation has caused the loss of more than 750,000 American jobs.

The sale of duplicated items that violate copyright – commonly known as 'piracy' – is now a massive worldwide industry. Unlike many other organised crime operations, the public are often quite supportive of piracy, viewing it (incorrectly) as a victimless crime. The argument is that the purchaser would not have bought the full-price item under any conditions, so purchasing a cut-price rip off does not cost the copyright owner a lost sale. Even when a sale clearly is lost, many people seem to think that the large profits that corporations make means that they somehow deserve to be stolen from. Most people are unaware, however, that professional pirates are organised criminals, and that the proceeds from the sale of copied videos, CDs, DVDs and software products are all fed back to supporting other organised crime activities. However you feel about corporate interests, major transnational criminal organisations and terrorist groups make extensive use of the profits from piracy to fund a range of horrendous activities, from planting bombs to enslaving children.

The ethnic Vietnamese crime organisation 'Born To Kill' openly relies on the selling of counterfeit watches – particularly Rolex and Cartier – to fund their other activities. The organisation's head is said to estimate annual sales at $35 million. In Los Angeles, several Chinese Triad groups are engaged in producing significant amounts of pirate software, using the proceeds to fund purchases of plastic explosive, automatic weaponry and dynamite. They include the Four Seas Triad, the Wah Ching, and the Big Circle Boys. The Triads are notorious slavers. The Provisional IRA is long-established as a vendor of counterfeit perfumes, medicines and veterinary products on both sides of the Atlantic, along with copied films, music and software. The money generated goes to fund their continuing operations. The price of that pirate video is a *lot* higher than almost anyone realises.

Still, the financial figures are alarming enough. According to the International IP Alliance, the US copyright industries lost over $12 billion in 1998 as a direct result of copyright violation activity. That included over $500 million lost by the book industry, $1.5 billion lost by the film industry, the same again lost by the music industry, and $8 billion lost by the software industry. The Motion Picture Association of America estimates that around five million pirate videos were seized annually by police worldwide in 1996, along with video equipment capable of turning out well over 30 million videos a year. Meanwhile, one third of all CDs sold across the world are pirate copies, and the value of the market in pirate music CDs is estimated at over $4 billion annually, according to figures provided by the International Federation of the Phonographic Industry. The situation is even worse for computer software – almost forty per cent of all software installed worldwide has been pirated. The cost to the software industry over the last five years has been almost $60 billion.

While copyright theft covers duplicated data, duplicated objects more commonly fall under trademark theft, and are commonly known as fakes rather than as pirate copies. The ICC (International Chamber of Commerce) estimates that the sale of counterfeit goods makes up a staggering eight per cent of all trade globally – $200 billion a year. Internet sales probably account for over ten per cent of that activity. Ten major producers of clothing, footwear and sportswear surveyed by the International Trademark Association had combined yearly losses of some $2 billion resulting from trademark theft. US Customs saw an increase of almost a third in impounded illegal fake goods in 1999, setting a new record level. As figures become available for subsequent years, they are almost certain to reach new heights.

Proprietary processes and techniques are covered by patents – registered inventions, innovations, formulae and techniques that the patent holder (often the creator) has the sole right to use for a certain fixed term. That term is twenty years, for World Trade Organisation members, who are signed up to the 1995 Agreement on Trade-Related Aspects of Intellectual Property Rights. If exclusive rights to patents were not available, there would be no competitive advantage in developing new inventions, techniques or substances, and the pace of technological and scientific advance would slow down greatly. The great majority of scientific and medical research is now sponsored by business interests.

Organised crime is mainly interested in patent violation as a source of producing counterfeit medical drugs. A lot of patented medicines are extremely expensive – the downside of exclusivity is the right to fix prices – so cheap, illegal medications are very popular, particularly in poorer countries that cannot afford the prices charged by western pharmaceutical companies. The drugs industry is thought to lose more than $2 billion annually through bootleg medical sales, according to the Pharmaceutical Research and Manufacturers' Association. In 1997, the World Health Organisation estimated that at least seven per cent of the world's medicines are produced illegally. Unfortunately, few of them are produced properly. Some are other medicines fraudulently rebranded to look like the drug that they are supposed to be. Others are poorly manufactured, of weak or uncertain dosage, or may be mixed with other substances to pad them out. Some counterfeit medicine can pose a significant health risk. The most commonly faked pharmaceutical products include cancer, diabetes and AIDS drugs, dietary and coronary medications, birth control pills and Viagra.

IP theft is a global crime. Particularly notorious sources of pirate and counterfeit goods include Taiwan, Hong Kong and China – between them, the source of over half of all counterfeit and pirate goods stopped by US Customs – along with Singapore and Malaysia, the Ukraine, Israel, and Argentina, Brazil and Paraguay. Although most nations now have implemented legislation to help prevent copyright and trademark violation, few of them have the financial or political commitment necessary to cause any significant problems for the criminal organisations. In fact, some observers suspect that some countries are consciously lax in their enforcement of copyright laws because of the value of the industry to the national economy. To make matters worse, IP crimes may be quite obscure – far enough outside the experience of the average police officer to make sure that they often go unnoticed, or are handled incorrectly. Corrupt civil servants and politicians also weaken legal efforts to stamp down on IP theft.

HI-TECH CRIME

Business and commerce are steadily becoming more and more dependent on sophisticated technology in order to protect their interests. Advanced computer systems offer a number of vital security options. The flip side however is that as hi-tech security increases, it provides increasing opportunities for sophisticated criminal exploitation. Breeching modern high-security systems takes great skill, backed up with a whole raft of organisational and logistical operations. Major crime groups are some of the very few organisations that have the dedication and resources to pull it off. Making unauthorised use of computer banking systems to hide illicit or sensitive transactions is less challenging for the TCOs, but every bit as important. Computer crime is a lot safer than many traditional crimes, both in terms of immediate danger, and of the penalties involved. In fact, in many cases the criminals will be based outside the jurisdiction of authorities in the country where the crime is committed. In some cases, corrupt programmers and system security experts are paid to leave open specific security holes – 'back doors' – which will let criminals into the system. Newspaper reports in 2000 stated that an Italian crime organisation had been caught in the process of stealing European Union aid destined for Sicily. Corrupt bank employees and members of a telecoms company collaborated with the criminals to help them break into the bank's computers, set up a fake node on the inter-bank money transfer network, and divert money across. They had stolen over $100 million by the time they were discovered – and had been planning to steal almost $1 billion.

The new generation of international criminals is highly computer literate. They grew up in computer-friendly environments, and have a good understanding of the potential of modern technology. Hacking-related information is very easy to come by nowadays. There are a lot of public sources for computer security information. The Internet is an obvious example – with hundreds of websites, newsgroups and mailing lists distributing the very latest news on security weaknesses that hackers can make use of – known as 'exploits'. But there are also plenty of published books and articles that contain all sorts of useful information. With a modest budget for computer equipment and a little computer programming experience, it is very easy now to teach yourself extremely sophisticated hacking skills from scratch.

The great majority of hackers have playful intentions. They're not criminally motivated – they just enjoy the challenge, and the sense of thumbing their noses at the system. But professional criminals are also lurking around the hacker scene, making lethal use of all the tips and tricks being posted on the bulletin boards and chat rooms. The global nature of the Internet means that criminal organisations based in the UK can pass hacking information stored in the USA to teams of expert hackers in India and Russia in order to break into a South African bank system and steal money belonging to an Australian company, depositing it in a secret bank account in Hong Kong – a legislative nightmare for law enforcement officials.

The problem is compounded by old technology. Western banks and businesses have a habit of exporting large pieces of obsolete equipment to less advanced countries, whose needs may be more modest. While almost all major western institutions have highly advanced security systems, that is not necessarily true in other countries. Some make use of long-outdated systems, or have intrinsically weak security processes. Criminal hackers can make use of these weaknesses to get into supposedly secure systems – and sometimes into the international banking network itself. During November 1999, organised criminals used the Internet and phone-banking services to hack into a number of financial institutions and steal hundreds of thousands of dollars. At the time of writing, the perpetrators are still free.

In addition to criminal hacking, TCOs are making good use of computer technology to help with a huge range of other criminal activities. All phone and fax traffic is routinely scanned and monitored by international security agencies, but top-range encrypted data transmissions are effectively impossible to crack. Modern communications offer secure, untraceable and instantaneous message transfer, enabling criminals to co-ordinate complicated international crimes in perfect security. The sheer volume of legitimate commercial and personal emails and transactions being carried out on the net every day offers a further level of protection. Even illegal or prohibited items can be sold quite openly, because it is so hard to locate individual sites if you do not know that they are there. Some contraband vendors even brag openly that they have been on-line for years without being caught.

Finally, fraud also provides plenty of opportunities for high-tech criminals. Illegal credit card fraud is a huge business. Some credit card details are obtained on the Internet, from people who deal in them, by hacking customer details from commercial sites, or by setting up a fake e-commerce site and using the card information entered into that. Most, however, are randomly generated, using special programs that can duplicate the way that banks assign credit card numbers. These card generation programs are able to churn out tens of thousands of numbers per hour, many of which are already legitimately assigned. In this way, someone's credit card details can be seemingly stolen and used fraudulently, when in fact the card number is coincidental.

The FBI joined forces with the Computer Security Institute in 1998 to carry out a fraud losses survey. Two hundred and forty-one companies responded, and reported that the previous year had cost them a total of $11 million in computer-related frauds, $17 million in telecoms fraud – with criminals using a company's phone lines to make calls – and $33 million through theft of trade secrets. Overall, credit card fraud is thought to cost businesses more than $3 billion annually.

2. THE BIG BOYS

CHINESE ORGANISED CRIME: THE TRIADS

The Chinese criminal community has been dominated by Triad societies since the seventeenth century. Like many such societies, Triads have secret traditions of brotherhood, ritual initiation ceremonies and a strong sense of kinship. They stand among the most dangerous organisations in the world, and are associated with a wide range of illegal activities. Triads work anywhere there is a Chinese community – dealing primarily in drug smuggling and protection. It is to be noted that, according to police officials in Hong Kong, although Triads do share many characteristics with other organised 'mafias', such as their Russian counterpart, their methods are less violent and more subtle.

There are an estimated 50 Triad societies in total, mostly based in Hong Kong, although there are a few in Taiwan. The most important Chinese organisations such as the Sun Tee On and 14-K groups are branching out and expanding, with connections in the USA (notably California and New York) as well as in Europe, in places like London and Amsterdam. They are fierce competitors for the western heroin market but since they prefer to operate mostly within their own communities, using the methods that they have perfected, it is unlikely that Triads will ever pose a lethal threat to western criminal organisations.

The Triads have been part of Chinese life for several centuries in one form or another. They started out as a political movement which, in time, went sour. It all began in 1644, when the Ching emperor Shunzhi overthrew the Ming Dynasty, conquered Peking and established himself as ruler of China. According to legend, five Buddhist monks created secret societies whose purpose was to oust these usurpers and put the Ming Dynasty back in power. Their motto was 'Crush the Ching, establish the Ming'.

Because the Ching emperors were from Manchuria, in Northern China, the Southern Chinese perceived them as invaders. The reign of the Ching emperors was harsh and repressive, and during this period these early Triads acted as protectors for the people of Southern China. Their members were highly trained in martial arts, and in what would be called today 'intelligence warfare'.

These partisan societies soon started to use their fighting techniques and secretive methods for criminal purposes – first against Ching-friendly businesses, and then, as profits grew, against everyone. Arcane initiation rites were introduced, and intricate communication methods were put together to ensure the welfare of the Triads and to strengthen the loyalty of members toward the society. The term 'Triad' itself comes from a symbol found on a banner used during secret ceremonies, a sign symbolising the three Chinese mystical elements of Heaven, Earth and Man.

These secret societies were called upon to fight during some key rebellions against the Ching Dynasty between 1790 to 1865. These included the White Lotus Society rebellion in Szechuan, Shansi and Hupeh, the Cudgel rebellion in Kwangsi in 1847 to 1850, and the uprising in Kwangsi province in 1851 to 1865, during Hung Hsui Chuan's T'ai Ping rebellion. The West helped the Ching emperors crush the T'ai Ping rebellion, which was largely organised by Hung, who called himself the brother of Christ. In Peking, the famous Boxer rebellion in 1900–01 saw the involvement of the White Lotus Society, but also of that of various other Triads such as the 'Red Fist' and the 'Big Swords'. At the top political levels, Sun Yat Sen, the founder of Republican China, allied himself to the Hsing Chung Triad in 1906.

Today, the Triads boast an army of members at least 80,000 strong. As in most criminal organisations, they have a strictly hierarchical structure. This is based on ranks and titles, as elsewhere, but also on numerical values that are assigned to roles according to arcane rules. At the top of the pyramid of power, the head of the organisation – sometimes referred to as the 'Dragon Head' – and his second in command, are people who can pass instant death judgement on members. The head of the Triad is known as either the *Tai-Lo*, which means Elder Brother, or the *Shan Chu* (Mountain Head) and is represented by the number 489. His immediate junior is either known as the *I-Lo* (Second Older Brother) or as the *Fu Shan Chu* (Second Mountain Head) and is represented by the number 438. At the same level of power, the Incense Master (or *Heung Chu*, also number 438), is responsible for the smooth running of the Triad's many rituals, and deals with the spiritual needs of new recruits. The Vanguard (*Sing Fung*) also holds the rank of the number 438, and is in charge of splinter groups of the Triad. He also helps out the Incense Master when need arises.

The commander of the troops is called the Red Pole (*Hung Kwan*) and his number is 426. He is responsible for the protection and the expansion of the Triad's turf. The financial and bureaucratic side of the Triads is under the rule of the White Paper Fan (*Pak Tzs Sin*), whose number is 415, while the liaison officer is called either *Cho Hai* – Grass Sandal – or more prosaically, Messenger. His number is 432. Common members are called *sze kau* (soldier) and are numbered 49.

The dignitaries form a ruling council. Beneath them, there are various quasi-military departments responsible for the Triad's operation:

- Communication: this service deals with the passing of information between different layers of the Triad's hierarchic system, between the individual members, and also liaison with other Triads.
- Operations: this department deals with the running of the Triad's activities such as prostitution, gambling, extortion, and drugs, as well as internal affairs such as punishments and revenge against other Triads.
- Accounting: handles financial matters such as money-laundering.
- Recruitment: this department organises social events and recruits new members and spies – and in some cases even sometimes forces people into becoming members.
- Training and welfare: The training wing employs a rigorous regime, to increase members' martial arts skills, weapons abilities and help them perfect their skills in other general criminal disciplines. There is also a welfare system, designed to take care of the members' widows, and wives of members currently behind bars, as well as providing medical insurance.

Although at first glance, the Triads might be seen as a highly hierarchical system resembling institutions such as the Italian Mafia, the way they work is noticeably different. For one thing, a Triad's way of operating is much looser and more relaxed than that of many other criminal organisations, and the activities of the members are not so rigidly controlled. A particular Triad does not always need permission from the Central Lodge in Hong Kong to carry on its own, more private, agenda. More important is the strong relationship between junior members *sai-los* (little brothers), offering loyalty, money and 'gifts' to senior members *dia-los* (big brothers), who in return give protection and information. Rather than inflicting a strict, controlled organisation on its members, a Triad provides an international infrastructure, a huge worldwide network aimed at facilitating its members' criminal activities, much like any mainstream business association. As a former member of the 14K Triad testified to a US Senate Subcommittee in 1992:

'I was not required to pay any percentage of profits to the 14K leadership. Triads do not work that way. Triad members do favours for each other, provide introductions and assistance to each other, engage in criminal schemes with one another, but Triads generally do not have the kind of strictly disciplined organisational structure that other criminal groups like the Italian Mafia have. For example, a Triad member would not necessarily be required to get permission from the Dragon Head of his particular Triad in order to engage in a particular criminal undertaking even if the deal involved an outsider or even a member of another Triad. On the other hand, on the occasion of traditional Chinese holidays such as Chinese New Year, Triad members traditionally give gifts to their big brothers or uncles who often are office bearers in the Triads.'

Despite their informal structure, the Triads are serious players on the international crime scene with a strong presence in Rotterdam and London, cornering a good part of the lucrative heroin market. Around 15 of the estimated 50 Triads in Hong Kong are very active internationally. It is estimated that To Luen Shun, the big boss of the Sun Yee On Triad, commands in the vicinity of 50,000 *sze kaus* and does considerable amounts of highly profitable business in prostitution, drugs and contraband smuggling, drugs refinement and counterfeit currency, amongst other things.

JAPANESE ORGANISED CRIME: THE YAKUZA

The Yakuza syndicates are the main criminal organisations in Japan, counting around 110,000 members worldwide at the turn of the millennium. The Yakuza have three main branches: the Bakuto and the Tekiya – both of whom trace their origins back to the sixteenth or seventeenth centuries – and the Gurentai, who emerged in modern times.

Before the establishment of the Tokugawa Shogunate (1603–1867), Japan went through decades of turmoil and anarchy, similar to the days of the American Wild West. Thousands of samurai – warriors – found themselves without the noble sponsorship that was theirs by birthright. For the samurai, being without a master was the ultimate shame, because it suggested that the samurai had outlived the family he was sworn to protect. A masterless samurai was known as a ronin, a 'wave man'. Many of these ronin banded together in wandering groups called *kabuki-mono* (crazy ones) that terrorised the population. They earned their name as much for their gaudy clothing as because of their habit of carrying *katanas* (long swords), and extreme violence.

In response to the roaming ronin plundering Japan, towns and villages armed themselves and equipped groups called *machi-yokko* (servants of the towns), who were clerks, shopkeepers and farmers. A few were honourable ronin, but for the most part they were less skilled in the fighting arts than their tormentors. The *machi-yokko* were soon perceived as provincial heroes throughout Japan, filling a role much like the British folk stories of Robin Hood. The *machi-yokko* faded away into the background after the period of the *kabuki-mono*, to resurface during the eighteenth century – according to the Yakuza anyway – as the 'Bakuto', or organised professional gamblers. They were allegedly employed by the Emperor in order to win back a share of the wages he gave to construction workers. The Bakuto went on to form one of the main wings of the Yakuza.

The Bakuto contributed a lot to the Yakuza culture, including its name. The term comes from a losing hand of *Hanafuda*, a card game similar to Black Jack. High score is 19, so a hand that adds up to 20 is a loser. *Ya* (8), *Ku* (9) and *Za* (3) adds up to a losing hand. As such, it is good for nothing, and the term began to be applied to the Bakuto. They adopted the name as a badge of pride.

The Bakuto also gave the Yakuza its most famous ritual, that of the *yubitsame*, or the severing of the top joint of the little finger. Usually an act of contrition to the *Oyabun*, or a punishment for bad behaviour, *yubitsame* made it more difficult for a swordsman to use his weapon, and for a gambler to finesse the cards, so it represented a serious sacrifice on the part of the individual Bakuto. Further serious errors would frequently result in further mutilation.

Finally, the Bakuto members also brought the famous Yakuza tattoos into the organisation. Tattoos were originally a mark of infamy, as the Japanese police used to tattoo a black ring on a criminal's arm each time he committed an offence. In the criminal atmosphere of the Bakuto, these marks became similar to battle scars, to be worn with pride. The tattooed man was marked out indelibly, someone who did not fit in with society and its codes. Tattoos soon became a test of toughness, with members suffering almost 100 hours of continual pain as a full back tattoo was applied. Modern Yakuza remain heavily tattooed as a mark of strength, and many bosses have personalised designs – even whole-body ones in some cases – which their soldiers are also obliged to wear, as a mark of belonging.

The second branch of the Yakuza, the Tekiya, came together in the seventeenth century, during the Tokugawa Shogunate. Street peddlers, petty con-men and phoney salesmen (like the Snake Oil peddlers of the US), who had been preying on the general population for centuries, united for protection and mutual interest. The Tekiya organisations originally focused on broadly legal activities. These included the control of market stall allocation, providing protection to businesses in the markets, collecting rent and ensuring the flow of goods. However, they also engaged in a number of criminal practices, including racketeering, hiding criminals and fugitives from the authorities for a fee, and often fighting with other criminal groups over territory.

The Tekiya were given formal recognition by the Japanese authorities towards the middle of the eighteenth century, and officially charged with keeping order in the markets. The *oyabuns* or top bosses were even given an equivalent to military rank, allowing them to take a surname, and to carry two swords openly in the manner of the samurai. However, even at that time the Tekiya had a well-deserved reputation for lying about their products, selling sub-standard or even simply useless goods, and doing everything in their power to swindle the unwary.

The Meiji Restoration in 1867 saw the start of Japan's industrialisation, the formation of a more powerful central government and the opening up of the country to the West. The Yakuza were swift to follow the rapid changes Japan was going through, and set up businesses in construction and transport. The Bakuto, based as they were around illegal gambling operations, grew less rapidly than their brothers in arms the Tekiya, for the former's activities were illegal throughout, while the latter had at least an appearance of legality for their fraud operations. The next logical step was quickly made and the Yakuza started to develop an interest in politics, supporting and assisting certain officials. This was both to make use of the inherent influence of the political posts themselves, and as a way of avoiding sanctions by acquiring friends in high places.

In 1945, after the Second World War, American occupation enforced a food rationing system, which helped the Yakuza establish a strong black market network. The Americans tried to investigate their activities, but without any significant progress. Central government was still too weak and fractured after Japan's catastrophic defeat in the war to offer too much resistance to the growing power of the Yakuza. It was during this period that the Gurentai were born and the Yakuza developed fully fledged mob-like characteristics.

The third branch of the Yakuza, the Gurentai, were Japan's answer to the US Capone gang, and they effectively attained a high degree of success through violent extortion and black marketeering. Their membership was drawn from Japanese citizens repatriated from Chinese-held Manchuria and the unemployed. On an operational level, everyone now became a target, not just traditional groups such as vendors and rival gamblers.

The Yakuza syndicates gained so much power during the late fifties and early sixties that at one point they had more people at their disposal than the entire Japanese army – 184,000 members in around 5,200 gangs. Their growth rate during this period was almost 150 per cent. This marked the start of the Yakuza's heavy involvement in drug trafficking. The result, almost inevitably, was a series of turf wars. These lasted until an ultra-nationalist called Yoshio Kodama, security advisor to the occupation forces during 1948 to 1952, put a stop to the fighting. Kodama managed to broker a set of alliances and truces between the various gangs and factions in the interests of increasing Japanese domestic power against the occupation forces. Despite a number of violent episodes in the 1980s, this unity has managed to remain fairly intact ever since.

With origins that stretch right back to folklore, and because of their status as members of a secret society, the Yakuza are an accepted part of Japanese life and culture, even if they remain an unpopular one. They have also been helpful to various Japanese governments in the officials' fight against labour unions at certain times. Nowadays, they are estimated to number over 100,000 members across the world.

The internal coherence of the Yakuza has always remained strong thanks to a fierce paternal/filial (*oyabun/kobun*) relationship. The *oyabun* provides help, advice and protection to the *kobun*, who swears unquestioning fealty and gives service when called to. This relationship is symbolically recreated in initiation rituals that focus on the exchange of cups of sake – a milder form of the sorts of bloody fealty rituals that are associated with the Mafia and the Triads.

The Yakuza have added modern, highly lucrative trades to their traditional street crime operations – narcotics, hardcore pornography (which is illegal in Japan), money laundering, money lending, rigging sports events and auctions, smuggling and selling contraband and weapons, and of course politics. The Yamagushi-gumi is the most important Yakuza syndicate, with control of over 2,500 businesses at one point.

A rhombus-shaped lapel pin worn on the suit denotes membership. The Yamagushi-gumi alone has had an annual turnover of around $460 million. In the 1980s, it had in excess of a hundred bosses, who managed more than 500 gangs. A boss could expect to earn up to $130,000 dollars a year, while a syndicate head would be getting around $360,000.

Japanese Yakuza clans have also branched out and formed a whole network of international alliances and other relationships. They work regularly with the other major transnational criminal organisations, including the Triads, Colombian and Mexican drug cartels, and Mafia groups in Italy and America. They owe much of their recent success to their durability. The methods they use to run their organisation – which other TCOs and legitimate corporations alike regard with envy – haven't changed in more than 300 years. Yakuza organisation is still based on the *oyabun–kobun* relationship.

RUSSIAN ORGANISED CRIME: THE ORGANIZATSIYA

The Organizatsiya is the name given to the collective institution of organised crime in Russia. Within the Organizatsiya at large, *vory v zakone* ('thieves-in-law') are the dominant section, and are the most representative of other major TCO structures in terms of recruitment and methods. They are mostly young criminals – 86 per cent of them are aged between 30 and 40 – originating mainly from Russia and Georgia, who adhere to a strict code of conduct and who are not afraid of violence.

Compared to other major criminal organisations, the Organizatsiya is new. There was little organised crime in Russia before the eighteenth century, when loose criminal structures dating back to the reign of Peter the Great started to become more formal. At the time more than thirty thousand criminals were thought to be active on the streets of Moscow alone. They steadily organised themselves into gangs. Sloppy practices were tightened up and roles and ranks within the criminal fraternity were redefined. The criminals even developed a special code-language (or cant) of their own, *Fenia*, so that they could communicate safely. Following the revolution in 1917, many former tsarists were very unhappy with the new regime, and they tried to weaken the communist regime by organising the gangs further.

Young gang leaders were taught to follow a strict code that would serve to keep them as a destabilising political force – never to work, never to start a family, never to serve in the army, never to contribute to social welfare, never to testify against any criminals, and never to turn to the police. These political gangs were called *zhigani*, and they were the beginning of a formalised under-world. As the *zhigani* developed and gained wealth and power, a split occurred between the gangsters who wanted social status, and others, who were content to remain in the shadows. Many of the latter criminals defected from the *zhigani* and set up independent groups, called *urki*, free from the burden of political agendas.

After many conflicts, a middle path between *zhigani* and *urki* was found – *the vory v zakone*, the blueprint for the modern Russian gangster. But another serious schism occurred during the Second World War. Some *vory* joined the armed forces, despite their pledge, while others kept their vows and ended up in jail. At the end of the war, those who had been to the front tried to rejoin the others, only to be branded as traitors and turned away. The result was a 'war of traitors', the *suchya voina*. The rejected thieves, who called themselves the *suki*, adopted a more lenient code than that of the *vory v zakone*, which allowed them to collaborate with the authorities. The *suki* were later used by Stalin to suppress his enemies within the gulags.

Much of the recruitment for the *vory v zakone* nowadays is carried out through the Russian prison system, and they continue to stick by their codes. Candidates gain membership after symbolic ceremonies and oaths, although there is no clear overall leadership. Differences also exist between various branches of the *vory* – between the Russian and Georgian groups for instance. The Georgians place great importance on the notion of family, and it is an inherent part of their alliances, as it is for the 'Ndrangheta faction of the Italian Mafia. Despite their differences, all of the *vory* obey a code of honour called *vorovskoi zakon*, similar to the original code of the *zhigani*, and also respect their own internal laws and procedures for dispensing judgement (*vorovskaia spravedlivost*). There is even a welfare fund, the *obshchak*, for thieves in need and their families. Attitudes have changed somewhat, though. Jail time was once considered an honour, a demonstration of fealty to the *vory v zakone* code. Now it is seen as a horrible inconvenience, with no status attached. Similarly, while once no *vor* would ever own a house, now many live in opulent luxury, both in Russia and abroad.

The Organizatsiya is divided into four levels of control. The *vory* are the criminal aristocracy, running operations and keeping control of the groups. Below them, the *avtoritety* (authorities) are the next rung down the ladder, dealing with general criminal operations in the same way as the *vory*, but with less prestige. Further down still, the *deltcy* (operators) deal in fraud and financial crime, particularly that requiring a high level of technical expertise and the *kataly* (convicts) run illegal gambling halls. The lowest level are the *shesterki* (number sixes) who oversee all the basic business of the gang. Beneath the *shesterki*, the rank and file membership of the gang is subdivided into *muziki* (men), *pahany* (boys), *obizenneye* (insulted) and *opuscennye* (declassified).

Life for the *vory v zakone* is not without risks, as the day-to-day use of violence is a defining characteristic of Russian underground gangs, partly because of the lack of central control. Otari Vitalievich Kvantrishvili, one of Russia's most powerful bosses, was killed in 1995 just after securing a significant deal with Boris Yeltsin to open a major national sports centre. On the back of this deal, Otari had also sewn up a number of major construction and heavy industry contracts, although the link between the two remained unclear. It is suspected that he was killed by Serghej Timofeev – a.k.a. Silvestr – another highly ranked boss. Five months later, Silvestr himself was blown up while driving through Moscow. 'The man at the wheel was literally spread on the seats,' the *Moskovskij Komsomolets* newspaper reported at the time. Investigators believed that Silvestr's murder was ordered by Bobab, another powerful *vor*, in retaliation for Otari's murder.

Criminal investigators believe that the vast majority of all murders and attempted murders that take place within expatriate Russian communities in the West are matters of retribution or territorial conflicts linked directly to the Organizatsiya. In 1995, the New York State Organised Crime Task Force made a special examination of murders of Russians across New York, Pennsylvania and New Jersey. In every case, either the victim or the killer (or both) was thought to be a member of the Organizatsiya. According to the report into the investigation released by the Tri-State Joint Soviet-Émigré Organized Crime Project, the killings were almost all professionally executed. 'Those who carried out the attacks often used distractions, decoys, or other tricks to gain advantage over victims. Fifty-three homicides involved the use of guns, including automatic, semi-automatic and silencer equipped handguns. Victims were often shot either at close range . . . or from a moving vehicle.' Because of the violence and intimidation by the mobsters, it is usually impossible to find anyone prepared to testify or even co-operate in these investigations.

An unusual characteristic of the Organizatsiya is that it limits its involvement in traditional street crime, such as drug networks or money laundering. Instead, the groups specialise in contract murder, arson, kidnapping, extortion rackets and an extensive array of fraud schemes – forgery, fraudulent antiques dealing, Social Security scams, health care fraud systems and so on. They are now considered to be the largest criminal group engaged in credit card fraud in the USA.

The Organizatsiya has adapted well to the modern world, and is constantly finding new markets for its illegal activities. Banks and finance institutions are a recent source of new, large-scale operations. The bosses are spread around the globe, mainly in the USA, France, Germany, Cyprus and Israel. There are signs that the *vory* are further organising themselves, too. After several summits in Prague during the early 1990s, the leading *vory* met in Vienna to discuss the future of the Organizatsiya after the collapse of communism. The meetings were held in accommodation provided by members of the Solntsevo syndicate, who had over several years purchased a series of restaurants, hotels, homes and shops in the centre of Vienna specifically for the meeting. If the Organizatsiya are unifying further, the results will be unpleasant for everyone.

ITALIAN ORGANISED CRIME: THE MAFIA

The Mafia is probably the most famous criminal organisation in the world, and it is certainly the most romanticised. It has even become an iconic part of American culture and history, idealised in endless television series and Hollywood movies, from *The Godfather* to *The Sopranos*. The truth, of course, is that there's very little to get misty-eyed about.

The origin of the Mafia is said to be a secret society in the ninth century, when Sicily was under the control of Arab forces. The local population fled the invaders and went up into the hills, where they built refuges – *mafia* means 'refuge' in Arabic. These refuges were used again every time Sicily was invaded thereafter – for example during the Norman invasion in the eleventh century. The Mafia was supposed to unite the local Sicilians against whichever group of invaders was oppressing the population. It was also to promote the Sicilian sense of identity and social values, such as family and cultural heritage. It had a highly hierarchical structure, based on chapters with lodges in the capital, Palermo.

Each chapter was controlled by a Don (the head of the family), who gave his loyalty to the Don of Dons in Palermo. Each member had to undergo symbolic initiation to prove his loyalty to the organisation, and to the five principles of the Mafia. The most famous of these vows was the vow of *omerta* – never to reveal any secrets or the identity of members under threat of death. The other vows included total obedience to the Don, assistance to fellow members, vengeance upon any wrongdoing inflicted on any member of the family, and avoidance of all contact with the authorities, who represented the invaders. This oath remains unchanged, and is still an important part of a new member's rite of passage.

As it grew in power and influence, the Mafia began turning its attention to criminal activities. This is documented as early as the sixteenth century, when the practice of passing out 'Black Hand' letters started. These were notes asking for protection money, and families who failed to pay were subject to violent retribution, kidnapping and even bombing. The status and power of the Mafia leaders expanded to such a degree that by 1876, Don Raffaele Palizzolo was able to force Sicily's voters to vote for him literally at gunpoint. He was duly elected into political office, and once in the government then had his friend Don Crispi elected to the post of Prime Minister of Sicily. The entire island came under Mafia control, and Palizzolo and Crispi began the wholesale diversion of government funds into gang coffers.

There was plenty of local opposition to this coup, but it was swiftly and savagely dealt with. Emanuel Notarbartelo was the Director of the Bank of Sicily when Palizzolo forced his way into power. Notarbartelo publicly promised to rid the country of the Mafiosi, but he was then assassinated in 1893. Don Palizzolo himself took over control of the bank. Although Notarbartelo's son later indicted Palizzolo, he was never in any real danger of being convicted. Prosecutors were unable to get witnesses to testify because of intimidation, and in some cases police files and documents went missing before making it to court.

Eager to try their hand at some new ventures, and fearing prosecution in their own country, Mafia members relocated to America during the big European exodus in the late nineteenth and early twentieth centuries. Many of them settled in New Orleans. The problem was first exposed in March 1891, when a vigilante group in New Orleans mobbed the local police jail and lynched several suspects being held for the murder of Police Chief David Hennessey. Hennessey had been investigating the murder of an Italian immigrant, and had discovered the presence of the Mafia. Following an extensive period of talking to Italian immigrants and even members of the police department back in Palermo, Hennessey had got to a point where he believed he was able to expose and destroy the New Orleans Mafia. He was killed before he was able to do so, however. More than a dozen suspects were arrested following a huge public outcry, before their lynching at the hands of a scared, angry mob.

This sparked a diplomatic incident between the USA and Italy, for the Italian ambassador demanded that the individuals responsible for the lynching in turn be brought to justice. The matter went all the way to the White House. President Harrison himself had to condemn the behaviour of the vigilantes. The families of the victims were paid $25 each. This affair did nothing to hinder the growth of the Mafia in the USA, and by 1900 every large American city had its own chapter, largely concentrating on extortion.

The prohibition era in the 1920s gave the Mafia a tremendous boost, enabling the Dons to extend their activities from protection schemes and extortion to prostitution, gambling and of course bootlegging. This was the time of the famous Mafia bosses such as Al Capone in Chicago and Charles 'Lucky' Luciano in New York, wielding their power with impunity. The next step came a few years later, when Luciano attempted to create a 'super Mafia', a syndicate to control and unify all the lodges in the USA, supported by the infamous 'Murder Inc.'. This latter organisation, consisting mainly of professional Jewish murderers, was for decades the contract killing arm of the US Mafia.

Luciano managed to unite the American Mafia families into one organisation, but the price was high. The majority of the original bosses on the board of the Syndicate ended up in jail or were murdered by rival factions, except Meyer Lansky, who remained in power until after World War II. Even so, the syndicate still controls Mafia affairs in the USA, and other branches of the organisation continue to exert influence all over the world.

Even though the likes of Hoffa and Al Capone belong to American history, the Mafia is still the biggest and strongest underground organisation in the USA. It is growing too, adapting to the information age and expanding its area of power to include South America and the Eastern bloc.

Despite the unity of the Syndicate in America and the Sicilian Mafia in Italy, there are actually hundreds of different Mafia-related organisations. The majority of these are small imitators based in Italy, many of them on Sicily itself. For the most part, they follow structures and habits similar to those of the significant groups, although some are actually organised as terrorist cell networks, with the head of each small gang knowing just one or two people outside his cell. The smaller groups will often co-operate with their larger cousins when asked to – not that they get a huge amount of choice in the matter.

After the Mafia, the Camorra and the 'Ndrangheta are the two most successful of the Italian criminal gangs. The Camorra originally developed from the Spanish secret society known as the Guarduna, which arose when the Kingdom of Naples was part of the Spanish Empire in the sixteenth century. Since then they have made Naples their base. Interestingly, the Camorra is steeped in the traditions of the Roman Catholic Church, using many of the Church's trappings within its own rituals and structures. However, this respect for the Church is hard to reconcile with an initiation ceremony that requires the candidate to carry out a ritual murder. A Grand Ruling Council governs the Camorra. Its long experience of smuggling tobacco and drugs has proved invaluable in recent years, when the items have become far more dangerous. With the collapse of the Eastern bloc, Russian weapons and nuclear material have come top of the Camorra shopping list.

The Fibbia and the Calabrian Mafia, the 'Ndrangheta – also known as the 'Honoured Society' – is the source of the legendary term 'Godfather'. From its early role as a resistance movement, it turned into a fully fledged criminal organisation. It quickly spread over to the USA, and was making use of Black Hand letters as early as 1906 in Pennsylvania. The 'Ndrangheta moved into drug dealing in the 1970s, and quickly gained international status in its own right. It is said to be dominated by the Sideno family – controlled by Comiso 'The Quail' Commisso – who have branches in Canada, the USA, Germany and Austria. The 'Ndrangheta is also involved in bribery, counterfeiting, kidnapping, theft and extortion, collaborates with the Colombian cartels, and has its own drug distribution network in Australia. In recent years, the 'Ndrangheta's activities have expanded to include arms trading and dumping nuclear waste, as well as significant investment in mainstream business ventures. The 'Ndrangheta makes heavy use of secret oaths, rituals and arcane ceremonies in the Calabrian dialect. Although it follows the same general ranking structure as most Mafia, its composite groups tend to be based on blood ties and marriage, which of course makes them far harder for the authorities to infiltrate. The 'Ndrangheta avoids the flashy lifestyle favoured by many other criminal groups, preferring to keep a low profile.

A relative newcomer to the Mafia landscape are the Sacra Corona Unita (United Sacred Crown), based in Puglia and said to be led by one Giuseppe Rogoli. The SCU maintains a fairly typical Mafia structure, although the titles it uses at the various ranks are not all identical. It specialises in prostitution and the slave trade, and has strong links to the Albanian crime groups. It also works with Russian and Chinese organised crime, and the Colombian and Mexican drugs cartels. The SCU are thought to have smuggled thousands of Albanians into Italy – many of them from the criminal underworld – along with a huge range of enslaved women from Russia, China and Albania for use as prostitutes.

Of the many smaller Mafia organisations, the Stidda (Star) are typical. A rural gang based in Sicily, the Stidda were set up purely as a profit-making organisation without any of the trappings of honour that the Mafia uses. Little is known about the Stidda's activities, which are thought to be limited. Members of the organisation receive a tattoo in the shape of a black and blue star between the thumb and first finger of their right hand, and are called *stiddari*. The Stidda compete directly with the Sicilian Mafia, and despite the murder of their leader, Calogero Lauria – he was blown up – they continue to be active.

The Mafia in general are highly regimented, with a tight internal political system based on rank. The highest authority of all is the Don of all the Dons, the 'Capo di Tutti Capi' – also known as the Capo Crimini, or Super Boss. He chairs the regular commission ('Cupola') meetings where international affairs and disputes between families are settled face to face between the collected Dons. Under the Capo Crimini are the individual Dons, sometimes also known as Capo (Boss), or Godfather. The Don is the head of a family, and his decisions regarding his family are final and absolute.

The Don's chief lieutenant is the Capo Bastone (underboss), also known as the Sotto Capo. He is the Don's chief enforcer and right arm, his voice and muscle, and is in charge of implementing the Don's decisions. The Capo Bastone and the Don are the only people permitted to swear new members into the family, and to hand out promotions and other positions of rank. The Consigliere, or counsellor, has the same rank as the Capo Bastone, but none of his effective power. His role is to provide recommendations and advice for the Don. Harking back to the court jesters of medieval times, the Consigliere is the only person allowed to speak his own mind at any time, even to the point of flatly contradicting or insulting the Don himself. He does not have any authority to override the Don's decisions, of course, but he does serve to keep the Don in check a little, and to point out obvious flaws in plans. Keeping an advisor of this sort is shrewd – if everyone around you is scared to contradict you, it is very easy to become egotistical, erratic, and sloppy. Many corporate chairmen could benefit greatly from a Consigliere.

Just below the Consigliere, the Contabile is the business advisor to the family, the accountant in charge of financial matters for the group. He acts only on orders, but can help provide advice in negotiating the maze of modern corporate finance. Two side ranks that report direct to the Don and the Capo Bastone come next in the chain of command. The 'Doberman', also known as the 'Hammer' or the 'Torpedo', is the family's most skilled assassin. He runs a crew of murderers, and takes care of the most difficult problems. He ranks alongside the 'Enforcers', who work solo for the Don as spies and scouts, and running special operations. Enforcers are permitted to operate in rival territory without molestation, as they represent the Don himself. These two positions are not found in all groups, and may originally have been specifically American mutations.

The Caporegime (literally 'boss of the group') is responsible for executing the family's individual operations. He has control of a crew, called a Borgáta, which is made up of several Capodecime ('boss of ten') and a number of soldiers. The Caporegime reports to the Consigliere or Capo Bastone to receive orders and directions, or to get permission to try a new operation. The Caporegime may also recommend specific people for membership in the family, as part of his crew. In most cases, the Caporegimes are effectively the heads of individual gangs operating at a street level. The Capodecime keep control over their men, and usually end up running operations out on the street. In some families, the Caporegime deal with soldiers directly, without the aid of Capodecimes.

The rank and file troops, soldati, are made up of sgarriste and picciotti. There is a great difference between these two ranks. Sgarriste, also known as wise guys, are sworn members of the family. Being 'made' into the family involves many oaths and ceremonies, and is the honour that all picciotti aspire to. It is the origin of the phrase 'made man' – once the soldier has been accepted into the family, he becomes entitled to far greater loyalty and security, and is entitled to progress in the organisation. The picciotti, also known as button men, are the lowest grade in the Mafia hierarchy. They have the potential to be accepted into the family, but their status is low, and they are not trusted. Picciotti are seen as expendable, and in any clash between a picciotto and a family member, the picciotto is automatically in the wrong.

The Mafia also frequently deals with people outside the family, both for complex operations and as extra muscle out on the street. These associates are known as giovane d'honore and are commonly referred to by full members as 'a friend of mine'. Although many crews include giovane d'honore as regulars, they are not – and will not – be part of the family, and have no influence whatsoever. Most giovane work directly for a sgarrista or picciotto, and help out in day-to-day street operations.

COLOMBIAN ORGANISED CRIME: THE DRUGS CARTELS

Unlike most organised criminal groups, the drugs cartels did not have any origins in historical resistance movements, either to fight off an oppressor, like the Mafia, or to provide defence against other criminals, like the Triads. The first cartel was set up in the 1970s, and based just outside the city of Medellin. Four men – Pablo Escobar, Jorge Luis Ochoa, Gonzalo Rodriguez Gacha and Carlos Lehder – dominated the Medellin cartel. The goal was simple right from the start – to smuggle as much cocaine as possible, at first from Bolivia to the USA, but soon to anywhere.

The profits were beyond the dreams of avarice, and the cartels quickly became rich and influential. Lehder started a newspaper and a political party while Escobar got himself elected to the Colombian parliament in 1982 and boasted a personal fortune of over $2 billion. He worked hard to come over as a philanthropist and personally financed the construction of an entire neighbourhood of Medellin in which 200 impoverished families lived.

The Medellin cartel did little to hide its activities, and in 1983 the group completed building a gigantic cocaine-processing factory in the Colombian hinterland called Tranquilandia. It had a private airstrip and road network, its own water and electricity, and included dormitories for workers. It was able to produce thousands of kilos of pure cocaine a month. Shortly after it came on line, Lara Bonilla, the Minister of Justice, started campaigning against the drugs trade, and in 1984 Tranquilandia was raided. The police arrested everyone working there, and confiscated weapons, several aircraft, chemicals, cars and an estimated fourteen tons of pure coke.

The heads of the Medellin cartel promptly disappeared, resurfacing in Panama. From there, they contacted the President of Colombia, Belisario Betancur, and offered a deal. It was simple and tempting – in exchange for immunity from prosecution, the cartel would pay off Colombia's entire foreign debt – about $13 billion – and invest their remaining personal capital in development programs. After some serious consideration – and, it is rumoured, following heavy international pressure – Betancur declined. The cartel continued their operations as usual, and instead invested heavily in land, industrial plants and mercenary armies.

The cartel assassinated Bonilla late in 1984. The government responded the following year by finally enforcing an extradition treaty that they had signed with the USA years earlier, and shipping four low-level traffickers to America to face justice. The cartel was furious, and started campaigning against the extradition treaty, under the slogan 'Better a grave in Colombia than a jail in the USA'. They even won a fair degree of popular support among the more nationalist segments of the population. The government refused to back down, however, and in 1986 the cartel started targeting prominent supporters of the extradition treaty. Late in 1986, they murdered Guillermo Cano, publisher of the capital's main newspaper *El Espectador*, and violence between the two governments and the drugs cartel started seriously to escalate.

After assassinating numerous law enforcement agents, judges and lobbyists, the cartel eventually went too far. They killed the Colombian Attorney-General, Carlos Mauro Hoyos Jiménez. The security forces responded by capturing Carlos Lehder with the help of the USA's Drug Enforcement Agency, and extraditing him to the States. The cartel retaliated by murdering the main presidential candidate, Luis Carlos Galan, in 1989. This touched off an all-out war, with the government efforts funded by American donations of $65 million. The government arrested countless traffickers, confiscated almost a thousand buildings and pieces of land, more than 700 vehicles, over 300 aircraft, almost a hundred boats, more than 1200 firearms, and almost five tons of cocaine. The cartel matched them strike for strike, bombing newspapers, banks, political parties, private homes and politicians' personal businesses. During the second half of 1989, they totally destroyed the *El Espectador* offices in September, destroyed an internal passenger jet in November killing 107 people, and devastated the national police agency in December.

Gonzalo Rodriguez Gacha was thought to be masterminding the terror campaign. Finally, after a gigantic manhunt, he was gunned down, and the cartel's remaining leaders – Jorge Luis Ochoa and his brothers, and Pablo Escobar – asked the government to negotiate. The compromise that they reached was that Escobar and the Ochoas would surrender and plead guilty, in return for guarantees that the extradition treaty would be scrapped, that they would be tried for just one general criminal offence, and that they would be housed in a prison on the outskirts of Medellin that they themselves would get built. The cartel leaders went to their five-star luxury prison, and the war stopped, although the flow of cocaine continued as normal. Meanwhile, as the Medellin cartel's leaders languished, a rival cartel based in the city of Cali was slowly gaining power.

A couple of years after his incarceration, in July 1992, Pablo Escobar escaped from his prison when the government decided to move him to a more secure unit. An elite unit of 1,500 soldiers was set on his trail, and over the following eighteen months most of Escobar's close associates were killed. Finally, the unit located and killed Escobar himself in December 1993. However, the drugs trade continued to grow.

With all of its attention fixed on Escobar and the remnants of the Medellin cartel, the Colombian government had been unable to stop the rise of other cartels, and America was still being flooded with cocaine at a rate of an estimated three tons a week. The Cali cartel, led by brothers Gilberto and Miguel Rodriguez-Orejuela, grew steadily more powerful over this period. It was considerably more discreet than the Medellin cartel had been and, by 1984, it was said to control over eighty per cent of all cocaine sales in New York, with a similarly dominant grip over the rest of the US and Europe. Where the Medellin cartel had been blatant in their activities, showing off their wealth and influence for all to see and living in luxury, the Cali cartel was more careful, and avoided open conflict with the authorities.

Even so, the reign of the Cali cartel was brief, broken between 1995 and 1996. The Rodriguez-Orejuelas were captured in 1995, and fellow boss Jose Santacruz-Londono was killed early in 1996. The final major Cali player, Pacho Herrera, surrendered in September 1996. Although the Cali cartel remains active, they have lost their dominance.

But that does not mean that drugs have stopped flowing, or that the Colombian cartels have been abandoned. The yearly Colombian export of 500 tons of cocaine – mainly from Medellin – is now handled by smaller gangs. Recent estimates suggest there are more than 40 cartels in Colombia, half of them within Medellin. The modern cartel leaders head up small, subtle organisations, wear quiet business suits and live exemplary lives. Seeing the result of open greed, they work in small groups, from easily portable labs, and retain their anonymity. They are decentralised, and use modern technologies, such as the Internet, to conduct their affairs.

The new cartels are less vicious than their predecessors, although they use violence when the need arises – although six anti-drugs investigators, almost certainly the victims of cartel hit squads, were killed over the course of 1998. They collaborate when necessary, and also work with political groups from both the revolutionary left and the paramilitary right, who use the drug money to fund their own political agendas. Production methods have changed, too. The cartels have recently invented a new compound known as 'black cocaine' – a form of the drug mixed with powdered iron and coal – that cannot be detected by sniffer dogs or standard chemical analysis. The black cocaine can be purified using simple solvents.

Despite the staggering cost of chasing after the cartels – both financial and human – the only result has been to break up a couple of big gangs and replace them with a lot of smaller ones. The flood of cocaine, meanwhile, continues to grow.

3. UP AND COMING ORGANISATIONS

BULGARIAN ORGANISED CRIME: THE MAFIYA

Bulgaria is home to a well-disciplined and organised domestic crime network. Like many of its former Soviet bloc neighbours, Bulgaria had a rough passage from communism to capitalism. Bulgaria's Mafiya has grown directly out of the ending of the cold war and the dissolution of the Soviet Union. The organisation is clearly divided into criminals from one of three specific backgrounds, and they each have their own interests, talents and historical perspectives.

The first group, consisting of former athletes, is a bizarre testament to the efficiency of communist sports organisation during the whole Cold War period. Their secluded lifestyles led them to form tight-knit groups and made them physically strong. The second group is made up of ex-policemen and secret agents from the communist era, especially those who got a head start in the free-market economy by being party to classified information about the economies of the West. The last group is comprised of members of the state-run civil service, called the *nomenklatura* in the days of communism. These individuals gained a vital understanding of procedures, official systems and bureaucracy. According to many observers, these three groups work together to run virtually the entire country on a criminal basis, and generate billions of dollars in profit. They do not restrict their activities to Bulgaria alone, either – the Mafiya has made its presence known throughout the European Union and Scandinavia.

Now approaching middle age, the former athletes of communist Bulgaria are a particularly interesting group of criminals. At the height of their training, these men were literally locked away together, and only allowed to work at their chosen Olympic sport. Failure in competition brought severe punishment. They went through all manner of success, failure, injury and adversity together. All the time they were looked after by the state.

When Communism crumbled in Bulgaria in 1989, these highly disciplined, super-fit athletes suddenly found themselves on the scrapheap. Most were resentful about being treated so poorly after the conditions that they had been forced to endure for 'the good of the state'. No one else had any jobs to offer them that would have allowed them to stay together, so the athletes turned to crime. If they had been taught anything by their Communist teachers, it was to act decisively and swiftly, which they did. The brighter members recognised that their teamwork and athletic expertise could be profitably used for criminal ends. The groups stayed together in cells, swiftly linking up into much larger groups to increase resources, safety and profits. Criminal activity started in dribs and drabs, but the early groups were successful, and word spread through the ranks of Bulgaria's former athletes.

One extended group fought for and took control of a chain of motels that can be found along the country's international freeways. This involved developing a wide variety of moneymaking schemes that would benefit from a high turnover of people and make a reasonable profit. The passing trade along the motorways facilitated ventures such as prostitution, drugs sales and money laundering, as well as overtly violent schemes such as armed robbery. Transients were the main targets – the Bulgarian motorways are the primary route to and from home for thousands of Turkish migrant workers, many of whom bring many months' worth of wages home with them in one journey. Western tourists were largely left alone, as possible reprisals were far higher.

The gangsters were used to travelling as athletes, and they carried on doing so as criminal businessmen. Because of their frequent trips to international competitions, they already had links with a fair number of border guards, and post-1989, the groups made a conscious effort to further befriend border patrols – or at least to become known to them. The benefits of being able to get goods in and out of the country quickly and without fuss were plain, and many athletes had already indulged in small-scale smuggling during their earlier careers. As these links developed, the trade routes opened – cars became one of Bulgaria's largest exports almost overnight, and the owners usually knew nothing about it.

After automobile theft, the Mafiya turned to racketeering. Success in sport requires focus, confidence, aggression and dedication, developed over years of mental discipline and physical training. Racketeering requires much the same qualities, and the former athletes threw themselves into it. As soon as free-market businesses began to emerge, the groups began to extort protection money from them.

Only the very tiniest fraction of extortion cases are reported, particularly in areas where local law enforcement is in chaos and the state is weak. It is simply far too risky to complain to officials who may be in the pay of the criminals already, and who do not have the resources to help even if they wanted to. Even so, official figures for organised extortion multiplied by 30 times during the first few years of the 1990s. In 1991, 21 complaints of racketeering were filed with the police; by 1996 there were 629. The movement toward democracy and a free market economy effectively brought with it not only government taxes, but also racketeering 'taxes' for the athlete gangs. Bulgaria's racketeering industry arose out of one of the first legal free-market business activities, gambling. As soon as the iron curtain collapsed, slot-machine gambling became very popular.

The government had not seen the need to put any legislation in place to control the location or spread of slot machines, and soon they were everywhere. Anyone with commercial public space was getting in on the act. This quickly led to disagreements over placement, ownership and market share, which disintegrated into territorial arguments. Disputes of these sorts are best won with the aid of strong-arm tactics. And the men with the strongest arms were the athletes. They took over other people's business disputes and supplied hired muscle to intimidate competitors. Once these rackets were established, the athletes moved from the gambling community to the general business world.

In order to give the rackets an appearance of legality, and to operate more openly, many of the gangs set up legitimate businesses involved in security, debt collection and insurance. These 'protection firms' prospered, with the police often unable to prove that the 'businesses' were just fronts for racketeering. These businesses could ply some of their trade openly, hanging extortion on the back of other legitimate related services. Meanwhile, the Mafiya was able to take advantage of a dramatic market development: the sudden emergence of a pressing need for unscrupulous debt collectors.

A popular scam between 1992 and 1994 was to borrow money from a financial body and then simply not pay it back. At that time Bulgaria suffered from crazy inflation levels. The scam was simple: borrow money, knowing that the banks were too weak and badly organised to make adequate checks, and then refuse to pay it back until threatened by an overloaded and painfully slow judicial system. Because of inflation, by that time the loan would be worth a fraction of its original value, and in many cases would not even be worth pursuing further. Given the disastrous situation, moneylenders turned to the newly established protection firms to help them out. By ensuring that the debts were paid – by hook or by crook – the protection firms earned themselves a tidy percentage of the owed sum, and they were sure to collect *their* money. A protection firm typically charged up to one third of the original debt, but this was still much better for the banks than not getting any money back at all.

When Ljuben Berov's government (1992–1994) legislated to bring the protection racket under control, it was too little too late. The groups were already established, and had become useful to legitimate sectors of society. Former state-owned banks, anxious to avoid losing more money to bad debtors, set up their own 'credit adjustment' departments, employing protection firms that were already doing the job for others. Some banks used the criminal groups directly, without even bothering to pretend that they were hiring debt collection agents.

This 'free market' for unorthodox financial services gave the athletes links to another of the main organised criminal sectors, the former civil servants – who were able to provide the paperwork and management know-how to complement the athletes' muscle. Moreover, many ex-civil servants involved in corruption and insider dealing found themselves frequently requiring the assistance of the ex-athlete gangs. The athletes, in turn, were able to benefit from the specialised knowledge and government links that the civil servants maintained.

The Bulgarian state came under significant international pressure and was forced to act, and in the mid-1990s many protection firms found their licences revoked. With the benefit of the ex-civil servants' good advice, many transformed themselves into 'insurance companies' and embarked on a long, legally complicated series of name and status changes that helped the racketeers to hide their former businesses behind new ones.

One such company offered insurance to owners of expensive, German-made cars, but its real business was stealing these cars, and demanding ransom money from the owners for their return. This developed into a form of automotive extortion in which the criminals collected the ransom without bothering to steal the car at all. Then false papers were issued to show that the car had been stolen, so that the owner could reclaim the ransom money from regular insurers.

Many of the former athletes have now gained real social power, but they all try to keep a low profile. From their simple beginnings in motel crime, these men have penetrated deeper into Bulgarian society than even they could ever have thought possible. Following the privatisation of state factories, they took control of several food processing companies. This gives them a high degree of control over the entire agricultural products market. Certain commodities – one of which is sugar – are almost completely dominated by the criminal groups. Some of the athletes have even managed to use their old fame as sporting champions to get into politics at important levels, unleashing a wave of corruption, with the criminals able to award tenders and public contracts for services, import and export licences, and so on.

Meanwhile, another criminal group was evolving. In the years following the Bulgarian change to democracy, thousands of policemen were forced to resign from the force and found themselves having to make ends meet in the new free market. As ex-cops often will they turned to security-related work and private investigation. The newly unemployed police were aware of the host of new 'protection' and 'insurance' firms opening up around them. The ex-policemen's skills were well suited to these jobs, and old friends – and even old enemies – proved useful contacts as the whole crooked security industry started flourishing in the new economy. Some of them found work as consultants and security systems specialists with the newly emerging businesses – both criminal and legitimate – and others set up their own groups, shadowing the activities of the athlete gangs.

Unsurprisingly, there was a certain amount of friction. In the mid-1990s, conflicts started to develop between the protection firms run by former policemen and those run by former athletes. One of the worst disputes developed along the beaches of the Bulgarian coast. These resorts were some of the most lucrative hunting grounds of the emerging economy, both in terms of legitimate trade, and in a number of illegal enterprises. As well as legitimate tourist business, the seaside resorts were well known for their gambling, prostitution and drugs, all of which provided a rich source of income for the racketeers. For a number of months, the situation threatened to erupt in all-out gang warfare. But it was in everyone's interests to sort out the division of territory quickly in order to return to the serious business of making money, so territories were demarcated without too much bloodshed.

Many policemen set their sights higher than street-level protection rackets. During the Communist era, as part of the daily routine of institutional paranoia,

Bulgarian citizens were extensively spied upon. It turned out to be pretty easy to turn 40 years of state snooping into excellent ways of making money. In the new democratic era, the people who had been doing the watching and listening found themselves in high demand, in possession of all sorts of invaluable information that the new free-marketeers were keen to exploit. Some retained certain elements of their old spy network, and engaged in industrial espionage. Those who had been monitoring the powerful or the wealthy were in a strong position to make a lot of money for keeping certain unpleasant facts quietly hidden.

Some departments in the security forces had close links to businesses that had been set up by the Communist government outside Bulgaria itself. In the mid-1980s, certain domestic companies were encouraged to set up outside the Eastern Bloc, in an effort to provide hard currency for Soviet governments. As a result, a complicated system of filtering certain banned goods into the country developed, so that the people in power could benefit from the programme. Following the change to democracy, it was simple to those who knew the system and the routes to exploit their knowledge, using it for criminal activity rather than just simply bending the rules a little. Apparently, about $200 million were invested in around 250 joint ventures and trading companies, and their turnover by 1989 exceeded one billion dollars. These companies had been state-owned, and so were still open to manipulation. They had never needed to stick to even the loosest accounting guidelines, so the companies were ripe for fraudulent exploitation. The former agents who had dealt with these companies quickly became extremely rich.

One final way in which the ex-policemen took advantage of their contacts was by smuggling contraband. Alcohol and cigarettes were the most popular goods for illegal importation. The scam involved labelling goods as 'temporary import' items, which were only being brought into the country to be shipped out again elsewhere. That got round the need to pay duty on them. The goods were then quietly reclassified, and sold as normally imported, fully legal goods.

The third main source of Bulgaria's organised criminals were the *nomenklatura* – former civil servants. When the country moved to democracy, they found themselves in positions of considerable power thanks to their knowledge of the functioning of government, their understanding of economics and their influence over local commercial affairs.

Large companies and multinationals in the West have a surprising amount in common with the old Communist regimes. They constantly monitor their employees, they trust no one, and they have huge resources that can be deployed almost to suit the economic climate. In addition, directors running the large companies and the people running the Communist countries had much the same objectives – to control the market and the people, and to further their own ends.

The *nomenklatura* held a lot of power under communist rule, but it was nothing compared to the amounts they grabbed for themselves in the months and years afterwards. They used all of the know-how they gained under Soviet rule to fully exploit the free-market economy and line their own pockets. As the free markets began to open up slowly in the early 1990s, a wide range of new options for laundering stolen funds appeared; certain *nomenklatura* found themselves well placed to exploit this new opportunity. They diverted former Communist party funds away from their intended destinations and into private businesses through a staggering range of channels – including false invoicing; misappropriation of funds to personal accounts; using contacts abroad for cash transfers and money laundering; privatising state assets for a song; selling (or appropriating) exclusive trade rights to friendly firms in other countries; manipulating fixed pricing and supply chains to sell state goods to their own companies way below market value and then flogging them on to the private sector at a high price; or vice-versa; and buying from private firms at a very high price, then re-selling to an arm of the same firm at a very low one, in return for a good cut. Millions of pounds of funds were stolen in the first few years of the new state.

Privileged members of the civil service had been able to make profitable contacts in a number of international locations. Most of these contacts were with other former Communist countries, mainly Russia and other sections of the former Soviet Union. Using the now considerable funds at their disposal, these criminals set about re-establishing contacts. International trade opportunities flourished, and corrupt dealings allowed many of the *nomenklatura* to put the money they had already embezzled to work and make even bigger profits. The dirty cash was hidden in foreign bank accounts.

The *nomenklatura* were in a position to decide what happened to most of the state-owned assets. Assets were sold off dirt cheap to shell companies that belonged to the civil servant organising the sale. Friends, relatives and other shell company holders with newly set up private concerns received the most profitable contracts. The commissions put out by the civil service always found their way to people who could be trusted to make the most of the opportunity – and to pay handsomely for the privilege. The really big money started to come when the *nomenklatura* used the combination of private and state companies to bounce goods in and out of state ownership. The 'spider system', as it was known, almost bankrupted the entire country. Meanwhile, the *nomenklatura* enjoyed incredible wealth, with all of their money coming from the state and taxpayers. The system was ingenious, and surprisingly simple. Virtual monopolies, as already privatised by the former civil servants anyway, would sell their inputs – items, commodities, resources, whatever – to companies that were still owned by the state, which the *nomenklatura* also had controlled. These transactions were at grossly inflated prices. The state company then sold the output – the same goods they had just bought – to private purchasers at rock-bottom prices. Many *nomenklatura* in on the act would make sure they owned both private companies already, but even when that was not the case, there was more than enough money to line everyone's pockets.

The outcome was that the state companies lost huge amounts of money when dealing with the private concerns. To make up the shortfall, the *nomenklatura* had the state companies borrow money from new, independent banks. The state companies then defaulted on the loans and were chased for the debt, so the National Bank was obliged to use public money to bail out the state companies. The end result was that the stolen sums came straight out of the public purse. This scam bankrupted 14 Bulgarian banks – including the First Private Bank, First East International Bank, the Bank for Agricultural Credit and the Yambol bank – and threw the whole country into serious financial chaos. In just one month in 1996, Bulgarian credit institutions lost 11 billion levs (about $5 billion). That same year the Bulgarian MP Edvin Sougarev said, 'The banking system in Bulgaria is inherently vicious because it was created for the purpose of robbing the nation by those authorised to represent it. If there is anything unique in Bulgaria's so called "transition", it is the major role of the banking system in the transformation of the absolute political power of the former Communist party into economic power.'

When war broke out in former Yugoslavia, the Mafiya moved in quickly. With embargoes in place restricting trade to the former Yugoslavia, goods were scarce, and prices rose sharply. The criminal gangs made a fortune by smuggling many different types of goods into the area, but the really big profits lay in selling oil and arms to the warring parties. This highly profitable trade required the co-operation of all three wings of the Mafiya. The *nomenklatura* arranged the supply of goods that belonged to or were produced by the Bulgarian state, and the athletes used a variety of methods to cheaply obtain private supplies. The police used their blackmailers and sympathetic contacts to make sure that no one interfered, and that cargo was able to cross the borders without inspection, partly thanks to forged documents provided by the *nomenklatura*. The athletes provided physical security and persuasion wherever necessary, making sure that nothing went wrong. This system worked perfectly, and the amount of profit made during the war was astronomical.

The Mafiya learnt that lesson well, and has continued to integrate and develop ever-stronger alliances. It took Bulgaria little more than ten years to develop its own, unique system of organised crime, and the result is a formidable force that is always expanding its operations into the West, while Bulgaria itself continues to suffer.

JAMAICAN (DIS)ORGANISED CRIME: THE YARDIES

Jamaica's criminal gangs trace their roots back to the capital Kingston in the late 1960s. Known as Yardies, these gangs were well established by the mid-1970s partly thanks to the country's post-independence political turmoil. Local community leaders realised that many people were willing to use extreme tactics to 'encourage' or 'discourage' voting. Local political leaders were forced to surround themselves with bodyguards to protect them from over-zealous opponents. If necessary, these same guards would also become enforcers, persuading people to vote for the politician in question, sometimes with the help of a gun. At first these 'posses' were little more than street gangs, but the ruthlessness and violence with which enemies were dispatched was truly amazing. The word 'posse' is most commonly associated with the spaghetti westerns of the era, a popular film genre in the neighbourhoods of Kingston. The lawlessness of the posses in the films, and the gun culture they embraced, fitted all too well with what was happening in Jamaica at that time.

Although the original posses had a purpose – supporting particular politicians – this became lost fairly early on, as the 'dons' who led the gangs allied themselves to those whom they thought would benefit them most politically. The posses set themselves up in strongholds that they could defend with a vast array of weaponry. This ranged from simple knives and cleavers in the beginning to much more sophisticated arms, including fully automatic submachine guns, later. A posse's 'garrison' usually covered a set stretch of land in the city, and people would know when they were entering posse territory.

As might be expected, the worst time for inter-posse violence came when elections were held at local and national level in Kingston and in Jamaica during the 1970s. Two big posses were allied to opposing parties, the Jamaican Labour Party (JLP) and the People's National Party (PNP). Both posses had huge memberships and a lot of firearms. In the 1980 elections in Jamaica it is estimated that there were approximately one thousand politically related deaths, and tens of thousands of violent crimes against people and property, all directly linked to posse activity.

As the violence continued, the posses sought other ways of using their time and resources. Drug smuggling was the obvious employment for someone with political power, brute force and a readily available source of the drugs. All three were available to the dons and their posses. Marijuana was commonly grown in Jamaica, and the island was rapidly becoming a stop-off point for cocaine on its way from South America to the United States. As the gangs made more money, they began to wield more political power. Drug trafficking was much easier with political clout, and vice versa.

The posses, or garrison communities as they became, began to be known by their locations: Jones Town, Trench Town and Tivoli, for example, are all parts of Kingston and the names of posses. From time to time, wars erupted between opposing political factions as they jostled for power or simply more space in the city. Adding drugs to the mix just made everything more serious, and the authorities became involved on a frequent basis. A notable incident occurred in 1997 when government troops and police stormed the 'community' of Tivoli. Armoured cars and helicopters provided backup to hundreds of state police who took part in the raid. After nearly 24 hours of fighting the gangsters finally gave themselves up. Tivoli was special in that it was the last of the big communities to be raided, but smaller gangs are pursued on an almost daily basis as the government tries its hardest to keep the Yardies under control.

Despite these efforts, it would be fair to say that the politicians – the very people who created the original gangs to help them gain power – now find themselves utterly overshadowed in influence and political might by the leaders of the Yardie communities. These drug dons, as they have become known, now have the upper hand with politicians, who have to hire their services in order to survive. But the price for supporting a politician is high. He or she will be required to back drug-dealing interests in government. This gives the Yardies an enormous amount of power in the impoverished inner cities and beyond.

There are a number of individuals who blur the line as politicans-cum-gangsters, but the majority of dons are just straight criminals, engaging in illegal activity around the world. Lester 'Jim Brown' Coke was the leader of the Shower Posse, based in Kingston. Due to the 'disappear-ance' or 'expiration' of witnesses, Coke had been let off from fourteen previous charges of murder and countless other smaller misdemeanours back in the 1980s. By 1990 the Jamaican Police Force, with help from law enforcement officers from the United States of America, set out to catch the killer. They estimated that he had killed nearly 70 citizens and thirteen police officers in the last year, and that was in Jamaica alone. Coke was also wanted in the States for various offences, most of them violent crimes against people. Following a full-on gun battle between the police and Coke (with 60 of his posse), Coke was arrested. Days later, his son was shot in the street by one of the many rival posses in the city. This sparked violence all over Kingston as the two groups sought revenge. As this continued and police resources were diverted elsewhere, Coke himself was fatally involved in a fight at the prison and so escaped legal justice, including possible extradition to the US. Coke left three surviving sons, all involved in Yardie gangs.

Another example of Yardie influence is the freeing of Donald 'Zekes' Phipps. This occurred in late 1998, and clearly shows the amount of local power that individual dons can gather. Zekes was arrested on violent crimes charges and imprisoned. Straight away the citizens of his community reacted violently, looting, trashing buildings, and shooting. The police were not too worried at first, and seemed content to let the people take it out on their own property, but a significant crowd gathered and marched out of the district. The crowd made its way to the prison in which Zekes was incarcerated, and laid siege. As the situation became increasingly tense, the police had to accept that they were badly outnumbered and were forced to let their prisoner go. The events were a nasty surprise for the authorities, and since then the government has started a number of efforts to undermine the power of the dons – including educating people to the dangers of drug-related violence, and warning them about other sources of violent crime.

The big problem is that in the inner cities the dons wield more power than anyone else. In their own communities they benefit the local residents – they have to. The dons can keep order where the police are unable to, they can offer lucrative jobs – in the drug trade – and they have been known to throw street parties to get the populace on their side. In April of 1999, there were riots following the announcement of petrol tax increases. Police intervention only served to aggravate the people, and it wasn't until the self-styled 'community leaders' agreed to sign 'peace treaties' with the government in return for backing down that things calmed down again and the streets were cleared. The dons calmed the riots down and then had their troops keep a low profile. The security forces were immediately withdrawn – having nothing to do – and the streets were left to the forces of the 'community leaders'. Meanwhile, the dons gained face with the local citizens for having quelled the riot and forced the government to withdraw.

Inevitably, the Yardies moved abroad to increase their profit base almost as soon as they were established back home. Keeping mostly to English-speaking countries – primarily Canada, the USA and England – the posses have established themselves firmly in the drug-running cultures of the countries they have entered. Weapons and drugs are still their main areas of interest. Other popular moneymaking schemes that Jamaican criminals indulge in now include passport forgery, illegal or false money transfers and general community-based criminal behaviour. The individual posses frequently fight among themselves. They often band together to take on outside rivals, however, giving them an important edge and making their effective strength difficult to assess. The groups stay tight, and individuals are known to travel frequently. Known gang members are as likely to turn up in New York as they are in London, for example.

Yardies have a strict hierarchy. The don is at the top. He is the source of all power, and is responsible to no one. As for the rest of the posse, the closer a member is to the don, the higher up in the organisation he is. At the bottom of the hierarchy are children in their early teens or even younger who are, essentially, trainee gangsters. The grassroots aspects of the Yardie gangs are apparent, as all members socialise together frequently. Often it is the younger members of the gang who undertake the nastiest jobs – contract killing for example – for it is comparatively easy to get them into difficult or secure places, and they face milder punishments if caught.

Jamaican criminals were being arrested in the USA as early as 1979, mostly for possession of marijuana, but this soon escalated to cocaine, violent crime and murder. Currently it is estimated that there are roughly 20,000 active posse members at large in the United States. They are concentrated down the East Coast, and in Illinois, Indiana and Michigan. However, there are more and more reports of posse activity coming out of the West Coast too, notably Los Angeles. When Jamaican nationals are caught in the United States for violent or drug-related crimes, they are repatriated, but the weak prison and legal system back home, and the power of local dons in Jamaica, means that they will rarely be in prison for long.

Britain has a long history of Caribbean influence and a proud Jamaican community to go with it. This community is now suffering heavily, as a result of expanded Yardie influence. As of 2002, gun crime on the streets of London had risen as much as 800 per cent in the last five years, according to a police report. Much of this rise was specifically attributed to the Jamaican gangs. The vast majority of Yardie activity takes place in London, in poor, crime-ridden boroughs like Hackney and Lambeth. The increasing Yardie violence and predation is driven by cocaine consumption in the financial district of City of London, and by competition for the incredibly profitable crack trade. London Yardies have been heavily involved with both of these drugs for years, and the violence continues to escalate.

ALBANIAN ORGANISED CRIME: THE FARES

Now that the dust has settled over the Kosovan conflict of 1999–2001 and NATO has pulled out of Albania, all that is left is to decide who rules the country – *really* rules the country. Although a democratically elected government is in place, most people would agree that the real power is in the hands of the criminal organisations, more commonly known as the Fares. Originally small, tight-knit, clannish groups, the Fares made the most of the opportunities presented by the recent war and the subsequent general anarchy in the Balkans and Eastern Europe. As a result, the Fares have grown in affluence and influence beyond all recognition since the fall of Communism, and their power extends far further than the borders of Albania.

Having moved away from scavenging through neighbouring, war-torn Kosovo, the Fares are concentrating their resources on their primary occupation: smuggling. There is no other group in Europe that comes close to the smuggling power of these highly organised, ruthless criminals. Their enormous success in this trade began as the former Yugoslavia collapsed and became, on the one hand, a battleground for all sorts of ethnic groups, and on the other – with the absence of all well-organised law and order – a breeding ground for criminal behaviour. During the Balkan wars, the Fares made money at first from smuggling commodities such as tobacco, oil, guns, ammunition, hard and soft drugs. You name it, the Fares could bring it into or out of the theatre of war. But this was just the beginning; the conflict also produced a huge demand for the safe passage of human cargo. People were willing to pay large amounts of money for safe transit out of the war-torn territories. So lucrative did this smuggling venture become that the local police forces and the Albanian government turned a blind eye to the Fares' activities. Since then, the passage offered by the Fares has become more and more desirable to refugees for places much further afield than the Balkan States.

Before the conflict, estimates suggest that organised human smugglers were making around £2 billion to £3 billion every year, and these amounts are thought to have increased since 1998. These estimates represent the smuggling of paying individuals into the EU alone; but the trade spreads much further afield, with traffic going all the way to the United States. The cost to the individual for the risk of a better life as an impoverished refugee in France, Germany or England is around £600 for an adult body and as little as £150 for a child. These tend to be group rates – more is expected for smaller groups or 'special deliveries', and it depends on where you want to go. Cheaper destinations are Italy or France, which are closer and less well protected. Switzerland and England are more expensive. The smugglers constantly monitor border security changes throughout the continent; as soon as one point is strengthened, another with weaker security will be exploited. Given the number of EU countries that touch on Eastern Europe, keeping the borders sealed is almost impossible.

As the news media are reporting with alarming regularity, illegal immigration is becoming an enormous problem for many European Union countries. Unable practically to just turn people away, and finding it increasingly difficult to process the high number of new cases every year, a new department has been set up by Europol to address the problem of illegal border crossing. This highlights the critical issue: how to stop people illegally entering the EU at all, for once they have got into one country, they are entitled to free passage between all others without the need for identification papers. The exception, however, is the UK, which did not sign up to the EU open borders agreement.

Although smuggling humans is the largest source of income for the Fares, it is by no means their only one.

Their second biggest money earner is, of course, drugs. Roughly three quarters of the heroin market in Germany and Switzerland is said to be controlled by Albanians. Authorities in Scandinavian countries have seen that the majority of their illegal hard drugs are coming through Albania, and even the UK has noticed a marked increase in the amount of heroin that comes in from Eastern and Central Europe. Hundreds of billions of pounds' worth of opiates are shipped across the continent annually along a path now known as 'The Balkan Route'. Europol knows that this route is responsible for the delivery of the vast majority of illegal drugs that flood the streets of major cities throughout the European Union and beyond but preventing their movement along it is almost impossible. The route is surprisingly far-reaching, and is controlled by Albanian gangs all the way along the line. A big problem for the anti-drug squads – of which there are many – is that even if they make a bust and take care of one group, there's always another ready to step into the breech and take over where the last one left off. The products originate in Pakistan, mainly, and formerly Afghanistan – although recent events have temporarily put paid to that – and are shipped through Turkey, which spans the two continents, before being moved through Yugoslavia and the Czech and Slovak republics. It is then dispatched to its primary destinations, Switzerland and Germany, Spain and Italy, and France and the UK. Traffic between these last two countries, once complicated and near-impossible, has been much facilitated by the criminal influence over a handful of Albanian ferry ports – in particular Vlore. With so much cargo passing through so many ports, Customs and Excise face an almost impossible task. The number of 'booze-cruisers' loading their vans with cheap continental tobacco and alcohol has added to the problem. And, because the routes are well established and well trodden, the smarter gangs are doubling up on their investments: smuggled people can carry smuggled drugs.

The Fares work throughout Europe. Despite being split into many gangs, each team knows what is good for the health of the whole organisation. Apparently, a Leadership Council, which is still based in the home country, runs the Fares, but regional gangs are allowed to be fairly autonomous. Regional gangs are run by a committee that has representatives from each of the local Fares' families. It is notoriously difficult for outsiders to gain any information from members, even those arrested and facing long jail terms. As with much organised crime, this is one of the biggest sources of frustration for the authorities trying to police the problem. The strongest international links that the gangs have are with nearby Bulgaria and Turkey, sources of much income and business. Arrests of Albanian gang drug couriers reveal that they are most likely to use the services of individuals from the Czech Republic and Bulgaria to do their dirty work, rather than risking people from their home country.

The most disturbing link, perhaps, is between the Albanian gangs and Italy. In fact, the Calabrian Mafia moved its base of operations to the coastal Albanian town of Vlore in 1999 when they were temporarily forced to pull out of Italy itself. These partnerships are not without their problems, however. Some of the Albanian gangs are said to have taken control of the cities in northern Italy and begun ousting the local, indigenous criminals.

Albanian gang successes abroad are more than matched by their successes at home. In Vlore, official estimates suggest that more than ten per cent of the total population is involved in organised crime. It is perhaps not surprising, given the difference in income between the taxpaying citizens and the cash-in-hand-economy gangs. A single cargo truck's worth of legitimate goods would yield an average of about £10,000, but the same shipment of contraband would realise anything up to £300,000. And in a city where everybody's doing it, it is even harder to walk away from that kind of profit. This sort of profit does, of course, come at a price – as with any gang, once you're in you don't get out.

Another big source of domestic income and trade for the Fares is car theft. It is estimated that up to 75 per cent of the cars on Vlore's streets are stolen. Other gang-dominated cities are not far behind. Originally cars were stolen as vehicles for transporting goods small enough to fit in them: drugs, people or other merchandise. What better car to use than one that was stolen on the streets of Milan or Genoa? Once a car has been used for a couple of trips, it became too much of a risk to travel internationally again, but it was then offloaded, either to one of the couriers or to one of the all-too-willing buyers on the streets of Albania's cities. The gangs were quick to see the huge demand for stolen vehicles, and now cars are taken from all around Europe for immediate resale.

A big problem faced by ordinary Albanians is the lack of any type of organised crime control. Years of Communist rule have not been good to the country, or to society as a whole. It has, however, been good to organised crime. The country became a democracy in 1991, and just six years later the entire economy collapsed. It was obviously not going to be easy to return to a free market in a country that had for so long relied on oppressing the individual. The collapse of the economy saw an outbreak of rioting and civil unrest that set the tone for the years following. The country revolted in such great numbers that no political force has been able to really pick up the pieces afterwards – only the Fares.

The situation is aggravated by the fact that the government commands little public respect and has almost no authority. Employees of the state are still perceived as oppressive, intrusive and aggressively opposed to the rights of the individual. There is alleged corruption at every level of society. Zef Preci, Minister of the Economy and Privatisation in 2000, described Albania as 'one of the most corrupt countries in Europe'.

In a poll taken in 2001, 52 per cent of Albanians said they had had to bribe their physician to obtain medical treatment. Recent years have seen no end of scandal and intrigue. The police forces are rarely united and support from other branches of government is limited – even when arrests are made there is no guarantee that the accused will face trial, let alone receive a conviction. The type of police force needed in a former Communist state is vastly different to that needed by a long-established free-market economy, and money and training for the police is not forthcoming. On top of this, the money flying around the organised crime circles can easily find its way into the pockets of a poorly paid policeman if he is willing to turn a blind eye to certain events.

There is now a lot of money in Albania for one reason or another. Since the conflict ripped the country apart, humanitarian aid from the West has been forthcoming but, as is so often the case in politically unstable countries, it is not always the needy who receive what well-meaning neighbours have donated. One notorious practice has been the diversion of aid funds to private accounts held by government officials and their relatives. The western world has often made the mistake of lazily assuming that a cash injection can solve a broken society's problems. In Albania's case, at least, it has had the opposite effect, causing even more problems than the country was already beset with.

A new generation of Albanians is growing up knowing only a lawless, profoundly corrupt society. The fear is that this could continue for generations, as long as the West continues to simply pump money in rather than concentrating on first stabilising the country and then improving it. Until then, the gangs are going to have the upper hand, as corruption at all levels rules the entire country. The longer the situation continues without remedy, the more the rest of Europe should worry too. It is worth noting that in 2001 the National Criminal Investigation Service described Albanian gangs as 'the greatest emerging threat' in the UK today.

MEXICAN ORGANISED CRIME

For a long time, the Colombian drug cartels have made use of Mexican drug dealers. It began in the early 1990s when the cartels started to pay Juan Garcia Abrego – currently serving eleven life sentences in a Texan jail – in cocaine for his smuggling services, rather than in cash, as was usual. The arrangement was profitable for both sides, and quickly became common, but the cartels did not realise the financial power the Mexican gangs were gaining. The now-deceased Mexican clan leader Amado Carillo Fuentes even bypassed the Colombians and purchased raw materials directly from Peru and Bolivia. The Mexican groups also produce their own drugs; Mexican organisations are believed to synthesise most of the methamphetamine that is consumed in the USA.

The transition from drug runners to drug lords came in the early 1990s. The drugs that they earned as smugglers were sold at a steady profit, in an increasingly competitive market. Marijuana was already a common source of income for the gangs, so the step up to sales and distribution of harder drugs was not difficult. Increasing orders and ambitious expansion soon served to propel the Mexicans up to their current heights. They were significantly helped on their way by their geographical location. The Mexican border with the USA is more than 2,000 miles long and it is estimated that 70 per cent of all cocaine entering the USA does so through Mexico. It is impossible to police it all, let alone keep track of the tens of thousands of trucks, containers and people that cross it every day. The North America Free Trade Agreement (NAFTA), ratified in 1993, was a godsend for traffickers. The fact that under the NAFTA bill, police forces are allowed to inspect only one in ten containers crossing the border, doesn't help them control a constant flow of drug shipments.

Mexican organised crime remains entirely focused on drugs. From their small start smuggling soft drugs across the border to the United States, Mexican traffickers have grown into extremely wealthy and powerful drug barons, shifting hundreds of tons of cocaine and heroin to major cities across North America. While Mexican gangs were once just couriers for the big-time players from further south, they now control a significant part of the market. This is thanks in part to the disintegration of the powerful Colombian cartels into smaller, more secure units, but it would be a mistake to underestimate the Mexicans' own part in their rise.

The Mexican gangs control their own wide-reaching distribution network across the USA, using all sorts of hi-tech gadgetry for telecommunications and weaponry, all of it sourced in the United States. The groups are fiercely independent, but inter-gang warring is rare and taking care of rival nationalities and international investigators is a much higher priority. In fact, rival gangs do work together, albeit for short periods. Two or more gangs may join up temporarily to quickly take care of a group – domestic or foreign – that is getting too greedy, or that they feel is operating too casually.

They also unite forces when really big shipments are made. Billions of dollars' worth of drugs are shipped across the US/Mexico border, and the bigger the shipment the bigger the payoff. If a huge shipment can be safeguarded using the muscle and political influence of multiple gangs at the same time, everyone wins. In some parts of the USA, not content with just bypassing the Colombian influence, the Mexican gangs have declared open war against their fellow Latinos, and even successfully annihilated some of them. This has happened along the East Coast of the US in general, and Florida in particular.

The large amounts of money the gangs earn from drugs have allowed them to manipulate politicians, law enforcement agents and border guards alike. In a country with an already volatile political and economic situation, the most successful drug barons are much like regional warlords, in the same way as the Colombian Escobar used to be. Based in huge armed strongholds just south of the US/Mexico border, they direct operations in the north. They are effectively cut off from threatened legislation as they operate on a higher plane than the simple politics of the common electorate. The system is so evidently corrupt that there has even been pressure from certain United States law enforcement agencies to accuse the government of Mexico of aiding the drug trade. According to a *New York Times* report in May 1997, 'Some of Mexico's most prominent anti-drug operations of the past year were undertaken at the behest of Mexico's biggest drug baron, who had enlisted corrupt generals in his war against a competitor. Military officers have testified in secret court proceedings here.' However, Mexico has had a total change in government since then.

Mexican gangs are seen by the US Drug Enforcement Agency (DEA) as the biggest single threat to the rule of law in the United States. According to Thomas Constantine, Director of the DEA, 'Drug syndicate groups from Mexico have eclipsed organised crime groups from Colombia as the premier law enforcement threat facing the United States today.'

NIGERIAN ORGANISED CRIME

Nigerian criminal organisations started off as humble couriers for drugs traffickers. But once a reasonable amount of money was amassed by the couriers, they could take on extra people, fund their own activities, and start to run a dedicated operation. It takes a lot of money to move up the ladder, however, which is why drugs-related crime is still the easiest way for a group to move out of the small time.

The most common target of the Nigerian organised crime activity is South Africa, which remains the richest country on the African continent. Before the Nigerian crime groups got involved, South Africa had no significant hard drug problem, but now statistics are showing a marked rise in drug crime and the violence that always accompanies it. The criminals do not limit themselves to drugs, however. Once enough money has been amassed in the drug trade, it becomes possible to use the profits to make even more through a wide variety of common schemes – smuggling people across sensitive borders, money laundering, extortion rackets, and fraud. All of this is accomplished with the help of the creative corruption needed to make illegal businesses run smoothly.

Nigeria is politically unstable, and riddled with corruption at all levels. Most affairs are carried out on a basis of patronage. The organised crime groups have been able to buy power at home in Nigeria, making them all the more powerful when dealing abroad. Payments to senior officials can make many of their activities look almost legitimate when viewed by the unsuspecting eye. An 'official' seal can make the difference between the success and failure of an operation.

Many Nigerian gangs specialise in fraud and money laundering. The most famous scheme targets victims based primarily in the United States, Canada and Britain, and plays on people's greed. Someone pretending to be a relative (usually wife) of a leading businessman or army general, usually newly deceased, approaches the victim. The relative tells the victim that the deceased had accumulated a vast amount of money – tens of millions – through unspecified means, and that the relative wants to get at the money by taking it out of the country. The paperwork that can be provided always looks convincing. The process is apparently expensive, though, and needs a legitimate foreign transfer, so, in return for paying the fees – a thousand pounds or so – for getting to the money and acting as the transfer point, the relative will give the victim a whopping 10 per cent of the cash. If the victim pays up, there will be setback after setback, all of which require further sums of money. When the victim gets suspicious, the relative vanishes, never to be seen again. This particular fraud is estimated to cost people in the UK and USA more than two hundred million pounds every year. It is known as the 419 scheme, taking its name from the criminal code that identifies it in Nigeria.

In the West, Nigerian gangs concentrate on the cities of New York, Houston and London. On the African continent, they stay largely within South Africa. There are some advantages to remaining within the same continent, because although the potential victims have less money, the politicians and police officers are cheaper, and bribery cultures are common. The internal problems that South Africa already has also make it easier for the Nigerian criminals to work their scams.

When visiting the West, Nigerian gangs tend to concentrate on a range of frauds. Immigration fraud is popular. This usually involves obtaining a tourist visa, student visa or even resident visa from the American embassy or consulate in Nigeria. As the staff in these offices includes many locals, corruption is said to be common, and it is not particularly difficult to obtain a visa using forged or out-of-date documents. These documents certify that the applicant has the required level of financial stability to obtain the visa, regardless of the amounts of money that he or she actually has. Popular ways to obtain US visas once the financial paperwork has been sorted out include false marriage papers, false US passports and other IDs, and false claims of birth in the US Virgin Islands. Because of the lure of the comparatively rich life available in the United States, fraudulently obtained US passports and entry visas fetch a very high price on the open market.

Identification fraud is another common way of making money. In the United States, particularly, many useful forms of identification can be obtained without too much trouble. These include driver's licences, birth certificates, utility bills and a number of other identifiers. These can be got hold of easily by almost anyone with a reasonable command of the language, a few simple resources and a bit of know-how. Once the first pieces of valid identification have been obtained they can then be used to get hold of the trickier types of ID, and it becomes increasingly difficult for the authorities to spot the intruder. As the fraudulent identity gathers increasing legitimacy, the opportunities to abuse the system increase steadily. The social security number is the most sought-after resource because that entitles the bearer to work or to claim whatever benefits may be available. Once a false identity has been set up it can easily be sold for tens of thousands of dollars, and the gangs often have hundreds of identities in development at any one time.

Credit card fraud is popular with most organised criminal groups. Credit cards can be stolen, duplicated in shops by correctly wiring a swipe-card reader, generated randomly using programs that mimic the bank algorithms for creating numbers, or fraudulently obtained using fake application details. Getting hold of just the card details also works; these can be found by stealing people's rubbish (or mail) and looking for statements or swipes, by conning people into providing them, or by buying them from a corrupt insider at a firm that gets a lot of card sales. Once the details are obtained, it is easy to order goods for shipping to a different address to the one on the card – or to purchase items that don't need shipping, such as electronic purchases. Goods will usually be shipped home to Nigeria as soon as they arrive, ensuring that the credit card companies cannot reclaim them if the fraud is discovered. Telephone calling cards are also popular – the same security number for credit-based long-distance phone calls can be sold cheaply to hundreds of different buyers, and will usually stay active for a few days. Phone fraud like this is particularly popular within the wider Nigerian and other immigrant communities, who often cannot afford to phone their families back home any other way.

Basic forgery has declined in popularity, however. American Express travellers cheques were commonly forged in the 1980s and early 1990s, until the US government managed to locate and shut down a large number of Nigerian-run printing presses in the eastern and western United States. The advent of digital printing and advances in paper technology has actually heightened public and institutional awareness. Because currency forgery is now so potentially easy, it is guarded against much more carefully, and has become less popular with the crime groups as a result. Subtler types of forgery have taken its place, such as forging letters of credit from banks in the home country. These are used to set up fraudulent accounts in American banks, which are then bled dry.

Welfare stamp fraud lies at more or less the other end of the scale, but is still extremely popular. The criminals provide proof of American citizenship and use it to take advantage of the welfare benefits on offer. Subsidised housing, food and even cash payments can be obtained. If multiple passports or identification papers are used, an individual can generate a lot of profit for the criminal group. Because of the difficulties associated with policing handouts of this sort, the system has been open to abuse for years.

Life assurance fraud requires more planning and co-ordination, but each instance can yield a substantial amount of money. A fake identity is set up in the US or UK and worked until it is strong enough to be able to withstand basic scrutiny. Life assurance cover is purchased for the fake identity, and the false person takes a trip back to Nigeria. Once back home, the criminal purchases official government and police papers proving that the fake person has died, and compensation is claimed under the life assurance. All the paperwork will be in order so the claim is paid as a matter of routine. Similar schemes are also used to claim insurance for stolen cars, lost goods and samples, and so on. There has also been a recent upsurge in the number of fraudulent personal injury claims.

An even easier financial scam was popular with US-based Nigerian groups in the 1980s. It involved obtaining student loans and simply never paying them back. The federal government certified the loans, which meant that banks were less than vigilant about who they handed them out to; when someone defaulted, the only loser was the taxpayer. Under the circumstances, proof of citizenship was rarely demanded. If identification was required it wasn't too difficult to obtain. The huge losses associated with the scheme led to the government clamping down in the late 1980s and demanding proper verification of identity and full checks on student status – initially only for 'Nigerian-sounding' surnames, but later on for everyone. Student loan fraud in the mid to late 1980s was estimated to have cost the American taxpayers hundreds of millions of dollars.

The Nigerian criminal gangs are, in general, well organised. The biggest offer fraud training to new recruits as soon as they arrive in the United States or United Kingdom. Given the amounts of money on offer the lure is significant for youngsters with little cash and few prospects. Within a given group there tends to be little hierarchy, with everyone working on a number of schemes according to personal preference. Most gangs run multiple fraud and forgery operations, and also use general drug trafficking as the basic footing of the operation. Unlike many other organised criminal groups, the Nigerian gangs are not territorial; their creed appears to be 'if you can make money too, then make money'. Most of the gangs are mobile, and will react quickly if they become aware of any need to move to a new area. The distribution of different types of crime that the Nigerian gangs engage in also helps them to avoid capture; different government agencies tend to be focused on specific types of crimes, none of which really captures the mixture of frauds, forgeries and drugs-peddling that has prevailed with the Nigerian groups. This makes them hard to spot, and, if caught, harder to bring to justice.

TURKISH ORGANISED CRIME

After the Second World War, the global trade in opiate drugs was totally dominated by Turkey. By the early 1970s, however, the United States had brought so much pressure to bear on the country, that the Turkish government banned all cultivation of opium poppies and put serious effort into enforcing the prohibition. This stopped domestic production pretty much dead in its tracks, but the drugs gangs responded by bringing in the raw materials from Afghanistan and Pakistan, both of which had slack attitudes towards drug law enforcement. Raw ingredients were shipped in to the Turkish gangs, processed, and then distributed onwards with the help of the Italian Mafia. Corrupt officials in Bulgaria, who were able to provide a useful step in the path from east to west, also provided some assistance.

By the mid to late seventies, the larger cities of western Europe were being flooded with drugs that had come from the Asia through Turkey and Bulgaria. This took a fair amount of organisation in Turkey, because of the government's anti-drug stance, and this was the preserve of the 'Babas'. They had previously been responsible for growing the opiates but, when that was stopped, they took over in the refining and distribution of the imported raw opium. This period coincided with an explosion of popularity of heroin in western Europe – in England and West Germany, in particular. The number of heroin-related deaths in the two countries shot up over a three-year period in the mid 1970s.

Drug enforcement agencies in Europe have had a number of significant victories over the Turkish groups but, even so, these seem to be little more than a drop in the ocean. The trade is as strong as ever, and heroin continues to gain popularity throughout western Europe, the best indicator of which is a fall in price. Over the course of 2001, the price of heroin in the UK fell by almost 14 per cent to a new all-time low of £13,000 a kilo. The purity is increasing as well, which means that each kilo provides less street-level product. It is now at approximately 40 per cent purity, almost three times as concentrated as it was during the 1980s. Between the two factors, the market may well be growing by 25 or 30 per cent annually.

Until relatively recently, Turkish organised criminals have been forced to rely on alliances with criminal groups in other countries, particularly Italy and Bulgaria. However, as the nature of global trade has changed and international commerce has become easier, the Turkish organisations have extended their reach. Controlling the drugs pipeline from beginning to end is a lot more profitable than being a link in the chain, and the Babas have expanded their operations, striking out further and further from their homeland. They have also moved into other activities, both at home and abroad.

The natural expansion from a drugs base is into money laundering, prostitution and racketeering. These are the most obvious choices, because they dovetail well with a drugs operation; the profits from drugs have to be cleaned carefully, in order to keep the network safe. Additionally, many prostitutes are drug addicts and even petty dealers, and are already in contact with the drugs distributors. Finally, the bars and clubs that deal in drugs are vulnerable to extortion, because they have so much to hide. All three activities have become established forms of income for the Turkish groups both within Turkey itself and in Turkish ex-pat communities in Germany, Britain and Holland.

The Babas are turning their groups into tough, violent and ruthless organisations. Long-running feuds with the Kurds have encouraged the development of the situation. Gangs have been fighting, and therefore toughening up, for decades. Violence is nothing new to the Turkish groups.

Estimates suggest that up to three quarters of all the heroin that reaches Europe now comes from Turkey – all of that being channelled through the Babas. The Turks themselves tend not to get involved in the street-level distribution, however. They prefer to leave end distribution to their clients because of the dangers involved. Their clients generally include independent Turkish criminals, Albanians and local criminal gangs. The fact that there are significant ethnically Turkish communities in many of the main destination countries eases the process, and means that betrayal is much less likely. Like the Fares, the Babas tend to recruit gang members from friends and families of existing members to maintain security.

However, staying out of the front line of distribution does not necessarily mean that the Babas do not have a significant presence on the streets. The Turkish organisations gained a significant public profile in England at the end of the 1990s and into the new century, thanks in part at least to their involvement in a number of rather spectacular ritual murders. There seems to have been a conscious effort on the part of some of the Babas to actually raise their profiles in certain countries, which goes against the preferences of most criminal organisations.

Most of the victims of Turkish organised violence have been Turkish or Cypriot until quite recently. Now, however, the violence is changing focus towards other ethnic communities as the Babas form alliances both internally and externally in order to fend off the growing competition from Albanian and Pakistani drugs gangs. During 2001, a group of Turkish gangs in London united with a group of Nigerian organised criminals to defend a set of drugs distribution channels in South London. The Nigerians were selling heroin purchased from the Turkish groups, and when a gang of Yardies tried to take over the area, both parties were threatened. The two groups formed an alliance and launched a war that led to five deaths and at least 18 cases of attempted murder. The Turkish gangs have historically been quite cautious about using violence. Unlike some of the other criminal groups, such as the Organizatsiya, the Fares and the Yardies, who are notoriously trigger-happy, the Babas are wary of the added attention that guns bring. Consequently, they control the use of violence in their gangs very carefully. If they have to reconsider this policy in order to deal with the increasing savagery of the drugs industry, the results may be bloody.

4. THE RISE OF THE TRANSNATIONAL ORGANISATIONS

In the past twenty years, law enforcement agencies across the globe have documented remarkable changes in the nature of organised crime. While it was inevitable that gangs would undergo gradual change and revisions, no one predicted the rate at which these alterations could occur, or to what degree. As analysts and law enforcement personnel looked on, nothing less than a radical evolution was occurring. Society's old foes were taking on the guises of corporations, both in terms of their internal organisation, and through the whitewashing of their very identities.

This massive reinvention was a simple matter of survival in the face of the new and formidable threat posed by law enforcement agencies and other competitors. Since 1980, the West has experienced one of the largest influxes of new crime organisations ever recorded, and the established crime groups have been besieged by scores of newcomers encroaching upon their territory. These invaders brought with them new skills, new attitudes and brutal ambitions to carve out their own places. The established groups recognised the threat and knew that they had to adapt to survive. The result is the grim criminal landscape of the twenty-first century – a veritable new world order.

THE INVASION
In many ways, the established organised crime groups within the West represented the old guard or the status quo of the criminal landscape, particularly in the cosmopolitan criminal atmosphere of the United States.

Their roots often went back for centuries, and they had connections to almost all aspects of modern society. Groups such as the Italian mob had control over most of the underworld of the East Coast, with ties to organised labour and – allegedly – politics. The Chinese Triads, or Tongs, of the West Coast, many of whose founders were brought into the country as the work force for the railroads in the nineteenth century, enjoyed a stranglehold on vice. Other organisations whose power had apparently waned still exerted influence over a variety of communities, such as the Irish and Jewish mobs on the East Coast. These groups embodied all of the traditional aspects of organised crime: loyalty, codes of conduct for members, and brutal punishments for transgressions. They were also set in their ways, and poorly prepared for what was coming.

The wave of criminal immigration can be traced back to its beginnings in the late 1970s and earlier 1980s. It was caused by the high level of political instability in many regions of the globe, and by the ambition of ever-more powerful domestic criminals in these regions to find new markets. Criminals entered the West undetected, hidden within the majority of law-abiding fellow immigrants fleeing poverty and brutal ruling regimes. The United States and other countries of the western world had riches that were ripe for picking, and the invaders boldly imported their operations and began to carve out territory. Compared to the horrors of war, famine and oppressive government, the new criminals felt that the worst their enemies could dish out was insignificant. Law enforcement agencies and the established organised crime groups were viewed with a mixture of contempt and disrespect.

The newly imported organisations came in a variety of forms and from a number of origins, but the ambition

and violence with which they operated was unprece-
dented, and took the potential competitors off guard.
Members of Colombian drug cartels moved into the
southern US, setting up supply and distribution networks as they went. Many of their members were
already hardened soldiers, and proved to be more than
a match for their competitors. Meanwhile, Jamaican
criminal groups quickly gained a reputation for extreme
violence as they sought to force their way into the drug
trade along the East Coast. One of the common fates
they dealt out to competitors was known as 'jointing',
because the victim was hacked into portions like a
chicken, with the aid of a chainsaw. The Russian Mafia,
the Organizatsiya, fled the deteriorating situation in
Eastern Europe for greener pastures and made their first
appearance in the early 1980s. They quickly became
known for a casual use of extreme violence that was
unmatched by anybody else. If it so much as moved, it
seemed, the Russian mafia shot it full of holes. A myriad
of other organisations hailing from Latin America,
Eastern Europe and Asia also moved in to set up shop,
using violence to force their way into the existing drug
trades. The 1980s have been rightly characterised as the
most violent time in the history of the American
underworld, eclipsing even the famous public clashes
that occurred during Prohibition in the 1920s.

The reaction of the established organised crime
groups was utter shock, followed by wary observation.
While not strangers to violence by any means, the
degree of brutality with which the newcomers operated
was both intimidating and disturbing. Due to cultural
differences and arrogance, older criminal organisations
like the Italian Mafia and the Triads saw overt violence
as risky and somehow amateurish, since it drew
unwanted attention from law enforcement agencies. The

old groups had also been unwilling to involve outsiders in their business, either as partners or as victims, but the new groups had no such compunctions.

When new groups such as the Jamaican posse known as the Spanglers started to carve out a niche, innocent bystanders frequently became casualties or examples. When the established groups saw the way things were going, they mobilised their vast resources and connections and began quietly to fight back. After analysing the new competition, the established organised crime groups decided that their opponents had respectable strength but lacked any real staying power. In general, this proved to be an accurate assessment. The bulk of the new invaders failed to make it through to the twenty-first century.

But these leaner, meaner invaders gave the oldsters a run for their money. The new criminal groups had a number of advantages over their entrenched competition, ranging from simple numbers to new methods of thinking. Even with the massive resources of the existing organised crime groups, the influence of the newcomers could barely be blunted, because they had both momentum and backing from parent organisations. At first, there were also simply too many new competitors for the established groups to take on effectively.

The new groups also had an initial advantage in the audacity with which they were willing to operate. The sheer scale of their violence took the public, law enforcement, and the competition by surprise. This was not mere shock tactics but a genuine indication of their character and methodology, and it earned them a formidable reputation. The Spanglers were able to grab control of a number of prime city blocks in New York in a short amount of time solely through extreme violence. Fortunately the high profile natures of their operations – and a quickly growing body count – drew a heavy-handed response from the authorities, and they were taken out of commission. When a swift and severe reaction from law enforcement became the norm, other budding crime groups had to take a more low-key approach or meet the same fate.

Perhaps the most significant advantage of the invaders, though, was that they had a fresh approach to the business of crime. While the old guard remained steeped in tradition, the newcomers were happy to embrace the latest advances in technology and apply these to their ventures. This allowed them several critical improvements in communications and resource management, and brought their general infrastructure and distribution networks right up to the cutting edge. It was the first step towards a 'corporate' reorganisation of the underworld, and it was something that the established groups learned from.

Before law enforcement agencies had time to even notice, both old and new organised crime groups were suddenly making radical alterations. The changes involved more than just a simple facelift; they reached to the very core of the organisations themselves. For a start, it became far more difficult to identify their members and operatives. This was different to the usual operational adjustments any group has to make when entering new territories, and wasn't initially seen as being related to expansion. On the contrary, the established groups that law enforcers were aware of had appeared to be in decline after years of focused anti-crime attention.

In the past, the types of operations run by the established organised crime groups (and the methods they used) had invariably borne a clear stamp of the organisation's character. For instance, Italian mob groups were characterised by highly professional mannerisms, a particular code of conduct for members, and a preference for concentrating in certain areas of interest, such as racketeering and labour unions. But by the end of the twentieth century, these groups were proving that they were willing to change these features – essentially making a clear break with the past.

All the old operating methodologies were re-evaluated. This included codes of conduct for dealing with members and rivals, general methods of control of subsidiaries, and even the way that outside threats were addressed. The resulting changes were simultaneously out of character and yet completely in character for the groups – after all, right from their conception, their survival had been achieved through flexibility when necessary. Unfortunately, the changes brought instability and internal upheaval within the groups at a time when they were not prepared for it. The Mafia, who had once been legendary for their caution and restraint, was suddenly marked by a number of very open and violent actions, such as the public assassination of Paul Castellano in New York City in 1985, under the orders of the 'Teflon Don', John Gotti. This sudden increase of the level of violence associated with ordinary operations became a trend that continues today.

THE ETHNIC BARRIER

Most organised criminal groups are known for being ethnically consistent, with tradition restricting key positions to specific narrow ethnic divisions. In the late 1980s, this was changing as quickly as the organisations' methodology. For the first time, people who would have been considered only lay members were given the opportunity to rise into positions of authority and power.

The first groups actively to loosen their restrictions were the Chinese mobs in the urban centres of the West Coast and New York. The core membership of the Triads – and all their leaders – was always full-blooded Chinese who had proven their loyalty to the organisation through many years of service and sometimes prison time. But in the late 1980s, groups such as the On Leong and the Wah Ching Triads began to expand their affiliations rapidly through the active recruitment of a variety of non-Chinese Asian members into their ranks. While still avoiding recruitment of *gwailo* ('ghost man'), a term applied to westerners of all races, they incorporated numerous Korean and Vietnamese in their ranks. This gave rise to what have become known as Viet-Chang gangs, formidable forces in their own right.

The looser restrictions on membership and access to a deeper recruiting pool offered a simple increase in manpower, and a significant additional bonus. By being willing to incorporate members of other ethnic groups, the gangs were soon able to penetrate communities that had traditionally been closed to all outsiders. This is particularly important in communities made up of immigrants who remain isolated from the larger culture, yet represent viable targets for organised crime.

Ethnic and cultural barriers of this sort have always proved to be a serious obstacle for both law enforcement and organised crime. Some groups, such as the Russian Organizatsiya, were essentially impenetrable in the 1980s and early 1990s by government agents who lacked any knowledge of the culture and language. Loosening ethnic requirements allowed the organisations to effectively overcome this barrier. Law enforcement agents still operated under the mistaken belief that the ethnic restrictions were in place, which proved to be a significant problem for them at the time.

Initially, crime operations carried out by the new recruits gave the parent organisations a degree of immunity that was normally only found when they operated within their own ethnic communities. While law enforcement has been able to bring down smaller groups, their efforts are always greatly frustrated by cultural barriers. Few indictments have ever been brought against the parent organisations. This has only made the new recruits and larger organisations bolder, encouraging them to carry out increasingly open and violent crimes. The Organizatsiya and the Viet-Chang gangs are particularly noteworthy, since they regularly show off their contempt for the law.

While the police were unable to get ethnic communities to co-operate enough to root out the groups involved, older criminal organisations were able to apply quite a bit of pressure to the groups, and this often brought results. In one instance, two Asian street gangs known as the Ghost Shadows and the White Eagle got into a very public war over territory and drug dealerships. Under the ever-greater scrutiny of law enforcement and media groups, and with the public growing ever less happy, the Triads that controlled the gangs moved in and forced them to end open hostilities.

CORPORATE REORGANISATION
The fact that organisations such as the Triads and the Mafia survived the turbulent 1980s is a credit to their ability to react effectively to the threat. They did so by acknowledging the strengths of their opponents, and adapting to counter them without taking on any related destructive characteristics. While old traditions and methodologies were still respected – in particular by older members – they were no longer held in quite such inviolate regard as they once had been. They were more

like vision statements for the organisations. Operations, policies, and even relations to other groups became increasingly organised, streamlined and professional, along the lines of a successful corporate organisation.

Analysts initially assumed that the changes were only going to be cosmetic, but it soon became apparent that the organised crime groups were deeply committed to making whatever changes they felt were necessary to remain competitive. For the most part, visible changes were implemented slowly, while major changes in policy, membership, and occasionally leadership occurred in the background and away from the eyes of outsiders. The process carried a substantial risk both to group unity and to operations, and law enforcement agencies documented several splits within targeted crime groups. Unfortunately, none of the incidents resulted in weaknesses that could be used to cripple the organisations.

Almost all organised crime groups operate within a well-defined command structure, but it wasn't until the late twentieth century that the potential weaknesses of the structure were made truly apparent. The devastation wreaked upon the Italian mob families in New York by federal authorities since the mid 1970s has served as both a warning and an example of organisational failings. Although a lot of the damage was inflicted with the assistance of informers and good police work, the tendency of traditional crime family command structures to crumble after key arrests made them vulnerable.

The Italian crime organisations traditionally had a linear command structure from top to bottom, with a single individual known as a boss or capo running the operations. Below him would be another individual, the underboss, followed by a layer of captains, and then various lieutenants, soldiers and associates. This structure gives the family far more strength and reach than it would have under a looser regime. Tasks were delegated from the top down, with no direct connection between the subordinate who committed a given crime, and the person who actually ordered it. This has proven to be an effective insulation against prosecution, and is in fact similar to many corporate organisational models.

However, it has several intrinsic weaknesses. The most serious of these is a lack of redundancy in the command structure itself. Redundancy in this context means having different sections working independently within one organisation, so that if one part fails, the rest does not follow. This concept is used in building computer networks. The Mafia structure is fairly linear with few people on each level until you reach the street. Like a corporation that has pared back its staff too far, the Italian mob is vulnerable because if one link in the chain snaps, the whole edifice could collapse.

The mob also has a built-in vulnerability to infighting. For example, the position of underboss is the focus of fierce competition, since the underboss is expected to succeed the boss if he is removed. Some groups have attempted to address the problem by having several people share the position but, in these cases, the infighting just gets worse, and the risk of treachery to the boss increases. These problems have caused friction at various points in the past, and, in the case of the Gambino crime family of New York, competitive infighting led to its downfall. This organisational structure also places a strong emphasis upon personal honour and loyalty of the members. This is rarely taken as seriously as it should be by the younger members of the families, which has led to a lot of damaging testimony.

The Italian crime families have sought to eliminate their weaknesses, but continue to show an unwillingness to compromise their traditional structure. Instead, they have compensated through other means, mainly by putting administrative practices in place, embracing technology and building ties with groups that they normally would not associate with. Some Italian crime families – such as the Detroit mob – have even taken steps to completely disassociate themselves from criminal connections.

The Chinese Triads represent an interesting comparison to the Italian groups, since they embrace a completely different operating philosophy. While both the Italian criminal organisations and the Triads operate on an international scale, the Triads seldom import the entire organisation to a new country. New offshoots retain their original home as the primary base of operations.

The strength of the Triad organisations lies in the fact that it is the embodiment of redundancy. It is like an octopus with tentacles in all sectors of society. If a person, or even a whole team is taken out, then there will be others there to step in and carry on. With so many groups of associates working independently to commit crimes, it has proven impossible to trace activities back to the command chain and thereby lodge damaging indictments. The fact that these organisations keep their leaderships outside the countries where the crimes are committed also helps make them difficult to combat and, to date, the only successes of law enforcement agencies have been against individual crews, low-ranking members, and the associated street gangs that act as enforcers.

The problems that the Triads suffer from are closely related to internal strife rather than to their command structure. Triads encourage their members to form semi-independent factions that operate with little direct control from above, effectively creating crime organisations within the parent group. While their efforts sometimes suffer from a lack of co-ordination, the emphasis placed upon independence and teamwork between members of particular gangs is considered sufficient to prevent serious rifts. Problems have occurred when groups of aligned Triad members – sometimes referred to by western law enforcement as sets or crews – compete for the same territory or scheme. Despite the emphasis placed upon brotherhood by the parent organisation, such competition has led to bloody conflicts between factions, and these have proven devastating to the associated gangs and their foot soldiers. While this does not affect the parent organisations as a whole, conflicts persist, and draw increasing attention from law enforcement.

The Triads have taken few steps to alleviate these perceived organisational weaknesses beyond an increased frequency with which proven ranked members are directly assigned to oversee particularly complicated operations or negotiate truces. Their inability to rein in warring factions has proven to be one of their major failings. They seem to lack the ability to pressure the combatants effectively, and the response usually comes far too slowly to avoid undue attention and collateral damage. The backlash from the ethnic communities that often live in the war zone seems to remain a stronger motivation than the threat of any potential intervention by law enforcement.

Despite the weaknesses associated with the various criminal structures, internal organisation did not change much as the various TCOs adapted. Any organisation is going to have weaknesses. Instead, the established groups decided to turn towards pragmatism and innovation. They took a long, close look at their new competitors, and honed their operations along similar lines. Faced with the threat of sophisticated and techno-logically savvy international rivals, extinction could have been a very real possibility had the old groups not been willing to embrace change to the degree that they did. The key lay in globalisation.

GLOBALISATION

All of the major TCOs, both new and old, have successfully adapted to thrive at the international level. This reflects a significant change in their outlook. They discarded old prejudices and rivalries and started doing whatever was required to get the job done as effectively as possible – no matter who that meant dealing with, or how much new technology they had to learn. With careful preparation and the reallocation of resources, many have managed to cultivate a significant global presence.

When looking towards markets in the international scene, organised crime groups still tend to think of themselves as independent parties. However, they all now acknowledge the advantage of functioning like a corporation and taking advantage of working relation-ships with other groups for the sake of profit. Although this has encouraged stability and co-operation, it hasn't eliminated conflict entirely. While entire organisations are no longer commonly caught up in violent disagree-ments, their associated groups, gangs and subsidiaries still provide the most obvious benchmark of relations. Violence between rival parent organisations is still most commonly expressed in violence in the streets.

Beyond the obvious profit advantage offered by maintaining an international presence, organised crime has taken the opportunity to exert influence in the same way as legitimate corporations. These include swaying the political processes of countries in their favour, destabilising entire regions, and even dictating government policies. In 1997, Russian president Boris Yeltsin admitted that 'criminals have today brazenly entered the political arena and are dictating its laws, helped by corrupt officials'.

As the lines between criminal businesses and corrupt corporations blur, some TCOs are starting to gain a façade of legitimacy for their legal interests. This has allowed some to bridge the gap between the criminal and legal realms, and even to make the shift completely in a few instances. The Detroit mobs are a prime example of this sort of transformation. Having poured money into legal interests, they have become disassociated from their old illegal ventures – yet they still retain a degree of influence over them.

No matter how legitimate or whitewashed a global crime group becomes, none is ever likely to divorce itself from its origins. They remain devoted to the pursuit of profit, and have proven willing to acquire it through any means necessary. The bottom line is that criminal tactics are still the fastest and most effective route to business success. Despite their changing image, the use of violence remains their primary tool for dealing with obstacles and competition – and it is still increasing.

If an organised criminal group wants to move beyond its national borders, it has to incorporate a number of features. These require a level of sophistication and resources that all of the established groups already have, and are a necessary part of the transition to a corporate model. The groups that arose during the shakedown of the 1980s, yet failed to survive, were all missing one or more of these features. Proper organisational maturity is required to succeed in the transnational criminal marketplace. Making the leap requires leadership, internal reorganisation, good accounting and accountability, the use of technology, sound networking, and planned expansion in stages. Without these things, even the most expansionist groups are still doomed to failure in the long term.

Becoming a TCO begins with decisions at the top. The leadership must decide upon a set of realistic future goals for the organisation, and the best course to reach them. Depending upon the current sophistication of the group, this can range from a general set of ideas to an actual business plan. The details of these proposals are extremely valuable to both rivals and law enforcement agencies. As such, the aspiring organisation must now add the new threat of corporate espionage to its self-defence considerations. Additionally, the leaders must be willing and able to put the needs of the organisation ahead of their personal desires and instinctive urges. This involves sacrifice and self-discipline but goes hand in hand with the hope that the organisation is expected to outlive its current members. With a strong direction and solid, dedicated leadership, the crime group is on its way to becoming an active TCO.

The organisational structure of crime groups is often an initial weak point, and may require adjustments to make it viable on the international level. This may include the addition of extra layers of members to serve as insulation to protect the leadership from direct reprisals, from both law enforcement and rival organisations. Both deniability and anonymity are useful.

Contingency plans must also be formulated for worst-case scenarios in which the command chain is completely eliminated. One option is to implement a devolving chain of command that will allow the organisation to survive when under serious attack. Trusted members must be ready to be fast-tracked into emergency command positions. Redundancy in operation represents a second viable option. The organisation is rearranged to allow individual sections to survive independently when central leadership is removed. While the redundancy option provides a better degree of effective crisis-proofing, it is also more vulnerable during periods of internal strife. Since each section essentially has the capability to operate on its own, the threat of an ambitious leader creating a rift and fracturing the organisation can be very real. The Triad organisations actively encourage the formation of independent sets, and rely upon strong cultural ties and personal loyalty to ensure group cohesion. In groups that do not enjoy such traditional strength, the weakness this represents is normally held in check through a combination of strong leadership, greed, peer pressure and outright intimidation. Infiltrators within the rank and file who report directly to the organisations' heads can also go a long way towards reducing this sort of problem.

Some organisations have found a middle ground between devolving chains of command and basic redundancy systems by choosing a departmental structure for their operations. This closely mimics legitimate corporations, in which all operations in a given geographic area are overseen in a pyramid-like control scheme. The lowest level is the equivalent of a field office or lower department, and it concentrates on promoting the organisation's interests locally. This unit is subservient to the equivalent of a sectional office, that reports in turn to a regional office. At the top is the equivalent of a head office that oversees the operations of the departments under it.

It is also possible for a given organisation to maintain a pyramidal control scheme of this sort for each country it operates in, with all head offices reporting to a single entity in the organisation's country of origin. This method of control has also been modified further, so that each sectional or regional office has individual work groups assigned to cover individual tasks. Different groups can be restricted to specific parts of the business so that they do not develop the expertise required to threaten the larger group. Furthermore, several different departments can operate the same schemes in the same territory, so that if one goes rogue or gets busted, it only takes a part of the business with it. This has the added benefit that any group trying to become independent will find itself clashing immediately with people on the street already working that niche for its former parent – and who will therefore be better funded and better armed. This does somewhat reduce the profits of the operation, but it also makes the organisation far safer from both internal and external attacks.

Once a corporate model has been implemented, accurate business analysis and accounting of all of the organisation's activities becomes critical. Starting with the investments and resource allocations, accounting also has to extend to evaluating the organisation's activities for profitability. All established criminal organisations maintain good records so as to keep an eye on the flow of profits and prevent internal theft, but a full audit of this kind requires the sort of business analysis and ruthless lack of sentimentality associated with *bona fide* large corporations. Activities have to be ranked according to the profits they return after allowances are made for the cost in time and manpower. If some of the more profitable crimes could be expanded with more resources, these have to be freed up by culling the less profitable sections. Bloated parts of the business may need to be downsized. The organisation has to become as fit as possible.

International operations have to be fully trackable yet remain flexible enough to manipulate far greater resources than ever before – all while addressing the problems posed by a score of new variables. These include increased distances, the accountability of regional chapters, and assorted problems associated with the bypassing of international borders. Juggling these tasks can be daunting, but there is a considerable overlap with the needs of internal discipline enforcement. It is an accepted fact that if the organisation as a whole is to survive, members of all ranks have to be held accountable for their actions. In the situation where a given section or member is not performing well, or is in breach of duties to the parent organisation, the accountants are often the first to detect the problem.

The criminal organisations that have truly thrived on the international level have demonstrated a firm grasp of modern technology and a willingness to incorporate it into all aspects of their criminal enterprises. This represents one of the most significant differences between many of the organisations that entered the scene in the 1980s and the established groups that they were attempting to encroach upon. The older groups were not unfamiliar with the advantages of technology, nor were they Luddite by nature; they simply had not realised the degree to which new advances could be exploited. Learning by example, it didn't take them long to make the most of the new opportunities technology offered. They have benefited from secure, reliable and encrypted communications, advanced logistics, data manipulation, hacking and computer crime and entirely new forms of fraud made possible by the Internet.

Mobile phones, computers and the Internet are as much a part of the crime scene as they are a part of everyday life for ordinary citizens. Such conveniences have commonly provided organised crime groups with the ability to augment their daily operations by way of secure encoded communications and simplified and accurate bookkeeping. They are also the basis for many new enterprises. Hi-tech crime has proven extremely profitable for a variety of organised crime groups including the Japanese Yakuza, sections of the Russian Organizatsiya, various Triads, and Nigerian fraudsters. And by enabling them to monitor those who are investigating them – for example by intercepting communications – it has helped them to stay ahead of the authorities.

If an organisation is going to become successfully established as an international power, it needs to cement its position and operations within its base sphere of influence. Since this is done in measured steps, it can be accurately referred to as staged expansion. Borrowing further from the corporate model, the solid planning present in a thorough mission statement is necessary to address adequately the obstacles lying in the way of growth.

Once general command and control factors have been taken care of, the first obstacle is dealing with rival groups of equivalent strength at a national level. Wherever rival syndicates exist conflict will have taken place, and the two groups will probably have a violent history. If the ambitious organisation expects to expand effectively, definitive action must be taken to either consolidate or destroy rivals. There are four recognised methods by which an opposing group can be brought in line: domination, incorporation, alignment, and elimination. The choice depends upon the strength and resources that the organisation has at its disposal. All of them have their particular dangers, but starting down any of the paths is almost guaranteed to end in the effective eradication of at least one of the groups.

Of the four options, domination is the equivalent of what corporate jargon calls a 'hostile takeover'. This is the most popular method if the targeted rival is perceived to have valuable resources, but is seen as inferior in its defensive capabilities. The aggressive organisation will make use of offensive actions designed to erode, but not eliminate, the command structure of the rival group in order to take it over with as little damage as possible. It will usually be necessary to kill rival gang leaders without wiping out too much of the rank and file. Valuable resources such as caches of supplies, skilled personnel, and other adaptable materials must be spared. Domination represents the most hazardous of the options, since it forces the attacking organisation to effectively pull its punches, whilst the opposition has no such restrictions. Caution must be exercised in situations where a weaker group may have a network of alliances in place. Domination was the method that the Bloods used in Los Angeles to take over a number of smaller rivals during their rise to national power.

Incorporation is often the most peaceful of the four options. It is the corporate equivalent of a merger. Violence is not considered an effective tool. Using a combination of negotiation and intimidation, and by playing upon the potential advantages of incorporation, the organisation seeking to expand brings a targeted group under its control. Normally the identity of the aggressive group remains dominant, but some fusions have occurred where the final product is an entirely new organisation. Incorporation has a similar end result to domination, although aggressive action tends to be counterproductive. A rival group that is considered troublesome may be incorporated simply to eliminate the source of the problem. This is often the procedure that leads to the creation of subsidiary groups with strong connections to the original parent organisations. An example of this method is the incorporation of the Wah Ching, a formidable street gang, by the Six Companies Triad in San Francisco.

The third option is alignment, which is similar to incorporation but allows the two groups to remain independent. Essentially they form a partnership. When two rival groups have such closely matched capabilities that war would be too costly, and neither can be intimidated into entering incorporation, the only option may be to enter into an alliance. Both groups share in the profits and expansion while retaining their old identities and leadership. Old rivalries and hostilities must be put aside for this to succeed, and this is often smoothed out through a variety of concessions. In practice complicated treaties and charters are drafted that carry significant penalties for secession and regulate the adding of new members. An example of this sort of consolidated entity is the Chicago-based Folk Nation, an affiliation of aligned gangs working together to form a national power.

The last – and least favourable – option is that of elimination, whereby an organisation commits to the complete eradication of the rival group because it represents an insurmountable obstacle to expansion. This is accomplished through a marked surge of violence that often proves extremely costly to standard operations. It is also highly visible to law enforcement agencies, which have a proven track record of intervening in violent gang wars. Open hostility to remove a rival group is never taken lightly since it includes a number of serious risks: the action may fail to destroy the rival, the market that supports the organisations may become disrupted, or the instigating group may become so weakened that they become open to predation by other rivals. The past 20 years have shown that large established groups such as the Syndicate and the Crips street gang – now affiliating with the Folk Nation – do not commonly employ elimination techniques to expand. It usually remains the preserve of smaller organisations, such as sponsored street gangs, and groups such as the Jamaican posses and Viet Chang groups, who are often willing to completely eradicate an opponent. Individual Yardie gangs are known to regularly launch genocidal wars against rival dealerships in order to gain control of larger territories. But this tactic remains unfeasible for larger organisations.

As both new and old international organised criminal groups elevated themselves to full TCO status, they quickly gained objectives to match. Instead of focusing upon minor schemes that might reap profits of hundreds of thousands of dollars, their efforts became directed towards the dominance of entire regions, where they could begin to make hundreds of millions. Many of the major transnational organisations grew to the same sort of power and influence as the multinational corporations in a very short amount of time.

World politics and regional conflicts are far more important to large international organisations than they are to groups who focus upon operations within a single country's borders. Wars, embargoes and unrest are all factors that directly affect an international organisation's prospects for survival. It is vital that the emergent TCO consider these factors. The gang will need to devote resources to dealing with areas such as politics and even, to a degree, 'nation building' – areas that it never would have needed to consider in the past. The weight of the legitimate issues that the TCOs find themselves entangled with can often prove to be more demanding and expensive than the comparatively simple operation of running an expanding crime syndicate.

For example, as the Organizatsiya has risen to power in Russia, it has become responsible for providing for the nation's citizens in a way that the government cannot. As the TCOs destabilise the government and deplete the public purse, they discover that they themselves in turn have to do something to keep the public stable. If their interests are neglected, the TCO will quickly discover just how powerful an angry public can be. The major organisations have found that in order to build upon the populace's dissatisfaction with the government, they have to offer some degree of alternative. For many TCOs, this has meant shoring up the economy, providing jobs, and even backing limited social programs. For example, the city of Cali used to be the most prosperous in Colombia, thanks largely to the influx of cash from the cocaine trade; now that the drugs cartel has been broken, Cali has returned to poverty.

They have also been expected to spur permanent changes to improve the region, which has brought them into direct conflict with governments and countries alike. Gaining significant power in a region is always a two-edged sword. Many TCOs have had to finance what amounts to a public civil war as they have attempted to consolidate their gains and take influence and power from the ruling regime.

In the international arena, the worst threat to any criminal group remains its fellow organisations. As they grew in power and resources through the 1980s, the various rivals quickly began to act like rival nations in flux – squaring off to grab as much territory and resources as possible before the start of a war. Conflict and competition were inevitable, but direct aggressive actions have been avoided as much as possible. Borrowing from the corporate model that they all follow, a range of covert action, subterfuge, espionage, political manoeuvring and general diplomacy have become the methods for defining the relationships between them. Like most market sectors, the TCOs realised that the greatest profits come through co-operating, not fighting – a criminal equivalent of price-fixing. It is the willingness of these organisations to work together without conflict that makes them such a threat to world governments.

POINTS OF CONTENTION

As the crime groups developed their transnational interests, the standard resources that any business requires became the focus of an increasing potential for conflict. If a rising crime network is to survive, there are several resource areas that it must have reliable access to and control of. Raw materials and trade and distribution privileges are two of the paramount issues to be considered.

Raw materials are one of the most critical requirements of any group, and the source of many conflicts. Note that in criminal businesses, raw materials may also represent relatively intangible resources, such as government subsidies that can be fraudulently obtained, or wealthy families to be shaken down. Even so, many organisations make most of their money through the marketing of illicit materials, whether drugs, pirated software or music CDs, cheap knock-offs of designer products such as clothing and perfume, or even stolen industrial secrets. Most groups exhibit a degree of specialisation in the items they choose to traffic, with their livelihood being directly tied to the availability and quality of the raw materials. Without a dependable and plentiful supply of illicit products, the organisation is soon finished.

Numerous bloody supplies disputes have been documented, including particularly costly clashes among imported Hong Kong Triads in San Francisco and among drug cartels in Thailand's golden triangle. While the preferred arrangement is for raw materials to be under the group's direct control or that of a loyal subsidiary, this may not always be possible. In such situations, the syndicate requiring the supply is automatically placed in a dependent position – much like the western nations, who remain largely at the mercy of the OPEC countries for their supply of oil. Organisations that devote significant resources to controlling raw materials often lack the manpower and international connections to distribute their wares, however. By providing supplementary services such as processing, refinement, and distribution, groups that have little control of the product's origin can apply sufficient leverage to the relationship to stay dominant. To continue with the petrol analogy, these dominant partners are like the multi-national oil companies and shippers who maintain a stranglehold on the trade.

The second primary limiting resource consists of trade and distribution rights, which are closely tied to the control of both territory and supply. This particular issue is by far the greatest source of bloodshed, and tends to be the most visible expression of tension between rival groups. Very public examples have appeared in the media in recent years, ranging from the long-running feud between the LA based Crips and Bloods street gangs, the ongoing war between the Folk Nation and People's Nation in Chicago, and the carnage created by clashes of Triad-sponsored street gangs in New York. Were it not for such blatant outbreaks of hostility, it is likely that the average citizen would have remained largely unaware of the growing expansion of organised crime.

Organisations must be able to move their products effectively and securely from supply to processing, and on to distribution, in order to keep up their funds. Not all organisations are involved in managing the initial supply of the product. Some organisations divide operations into sections, each of which is only involved with one aspect of the supply chain. This is effectively similar to departmentalisation, where individual sub-groups are held responsible for particular duties. Distribution duties are normally left to the lower tiers of the organisation, such as the street gangs and low-level crews. This has several advantages for the TCO. Gang members tend to be considerably more knowledgeable about their home turf than other operators, and may have contacts and tricks that other agents would not. Their members are also easily exploited, and they are plentiful enough to be expendable. Acting on a street level carries a number of serious dangers with it, but since the parent organisation doesn't invest much in the individual gang members beyond relatively minor kick-backs, the high attrition rate they suffer is of no consequence. In the case of drug distribution, gang members are exploited to the same degree as the victims to whom they sell.

Distribution networks are the life-blood of all international criminal organisations, regardless of what they are selling, and are therefore fiercely defended. Whether the threat comes from a rival group, an internal rival or a law enforcement agency, the response is broadly the same. Individual cells in a distribution network possess a certain degree of independence from the TCO entity, and are expected to be able to deal with threats to their personal part of the network without any assistance. This can sometimes get out of hand as a particular sub-group may lack the restraint of its parent organisation. A particularly notorious example was the string of public massacres that took place in the late 1970s in San Francisco. A war erupted between two Triad-backed street gangs, the Wah Ching ('Chinese Youth') and the Joe Boys. Numerous innocents were caught in the crossfire as members of the two groups engaged in sporadic clashes. While many parent organisations remain largely unconcerned over the activities of the lay members manning the networks, swift and decisive action is always taken when the network's efficiency is jeopardised. With growing pressure from law enforcement, the Triads that sponsored the two gangs agreed to weigh in and halt the hostilities.

Distribution networks normally encompass three separate duties – transport, distribution, and sale. As with raw materials, these can sometimes represent entirely intangible issues. The actual mechanics of distribution vary greatly depending upon the product being sold and the level of sophistication of the participating organisations. In some cases, several crime groups working in unison may share duties to run the network, although they do not normally operate within the same geographic area. Relationships like these are most evident in drugs supply networks, which often stretch across the territories of as many as four or five different groups. A typical chain might see opium produced in Afghanistan by Pakistani cartels being sold to Turkish refiners, who then distribute the pure heroin to Bulgarian organisations. It then may be sold on again to Albanian street gangs in the UK, operating under the aegis of British firms.

INTERVENTION AND LEGISLATION

Given the importance of primary distribution networks to an organisation's survival, it is no great surprise that they are also the primary focus for law enforcement agencies seeking to suppress the criminal groups. Operations of this sort have formed the backbone of the struggle against organised crime – including the United States' well-known 'War on Drugs'. This is technically referred to as 'interdiction', and takes place on a variety of levels and fronts, much like the theatres of a military campaign. International borders are of little concern, since the measures employed are extensions of Western policies, and are organised and generally co-ordinated by Western agencies. These measures typically make use of resources and manpower in the resource's country of origin. In an effort to stop the cocaine trade at source during its War on Drugs, the United States government has brought all kinds of pressure to bear on Colombia – political, technical, military and fiscal. Despite the sweeping application of these policies, the programme has unfortunately proven to be a miserable failure. Like the organisations themselves, the drugs distribution business continues to get stronger and stronger.

By comparison – and as a good example of ever-greater global co-operation – the organised crime networks seldom engage in any real form of interdiction against their rivals. Although they may genuinely believe that the potential profits are substantial enough to go around, it is more likely that they lack the resources or desire to expand beyond a manageable rate – and that they know first-hand how ineffective these actions have been, for law enforcement agencies at least. Conflict between the major TCOs remains concentrated at street level, and is only really carried out by subsidiaries and sponsored forces.

First-level interdiction targets the geographic location where the illicit goods are produced or processed. With the support and guidance of sponsoring western nations, the native government is co-ordinated to take a number of aggressive actions against the resources that the organised crime groups control. This normally takes the form of direct military manoeuvres, but it can also include increased national security, and tighter restrictions on international travel and shipping. These operations receive large amounts of media attention and good publicity, and attract significant amounts of funding. However, as the operations against the Colombian cartels and several other regimes in Latin America clearly show, they have met with little genuine lasting success.

Second-level interdiction is designed to interrupt the flow of illicit goods from the processing and production centres as they are transported to the criminal organisation's distribution network. Good intelligence is key to this phase, since the contacts and channels that provide the links between sources and distribution must be identified and targeted. This is very similar to the preparations required for military actions designed to cut the supply lines of opposing forces during times of war. Intermediary countries that can be persuaded to assist tend to provide both the main arenas for action, and the primary resources – personnel, weapons and so on – used to interrupt the flow of goods. The process dovetails with the first level of interdiction, making co-ordination with the source country's forces a necessity.

Third-level interdiction – the final level – takes place in the countries that are the eventual receiving end of the distribution networks. It is here that the full resources of the nation sponsoring the action can be brought to bear. The process is characterised by massive increases in funding for law enforcement agencies, stricter legislation to penalise criminals, and some of the most violent reaction from the criminal organisations to date. Although the sponsoring government would appear to have the advantage, the crime organisations are often so deeply entrenched that they cannot be effectively excised. The TCOs are simply too deeply woven into our societies to shake out easily. The primary risk of interdiction at this level is that the conflicts tend to occur on the streets rather than in remote areas, and so carry a high potential for the loss of innocent life.

The worst possible result of forceful action against international crime organisations is that the group actually ends up benefiting from the mayhem. Nietzsche famously said 'that which does not kill me makes me stronger', and international criminal networks have shown that they have the resilience not only to thrive but actually expand under the pressure of global law enforcement initiatives. The past 20 years have clearly demonstrated that although concerted interdiction policies have occasionally managed to disrupt both networks and supply lines, the groups' use of redundant structures and supply schemes has allowed them to largely operate without interruption. In some cases – such as that of several Yakuza organisations – the action provided the opportunity to open new markets, and the organisations have actually profited. Other repercussions have included the effect witnessed during Prohibition in America in the 1920s, where restrictions on products allowed organised crime groups to dramatically drive up the prices of illicit goods and increase their power. The sad truth is that interdiction has created vast profits for the TCOs, making the War on Drugs one of the best things that ever happened to them.

THE NEW CRIMINAL ORDER
Transnational organised crime has reached the level where the participants are effectively operating as lean,

hungry business conglomerates. Although the syndicates acknowledge their origins, they have grown to the point that they now have little in common with the less advanced groups that are limited within national boundaries. It could be said that the difference comes from the shared power and vision of the TCOs, but it is also a function of the level of sophistication with which they operate.

The international criminal syndicates have moved far beyond their origins as street gangs and enforcers. On the street the same assembly of thugs, killers, hard men and drug peddlers continue to promote the parent organisation's interests, but their role in the ongoing development of the organisation is minimal. They are just another resource. With the average syndicate having the capability to maintain well-defined distribution networks in scores of countries and on multiple continents at once, the fate and contribution of an individual member is almost totally irrelevant.

The true indicator that such organisations have moved beyond their roots as gangs or small criminal rings is their willingness to shelve old rivalries and work together towards common ends. This has gone beyond simple concerns of survival and developed into genuine professionalism, in which former rivals are treated like potential partners. This is not to say that conflict has been given up entirely – just that it occurs in different forms. Diplomacy and negotiation skills remain the preferred tools with which to resolve problems. Resilient business relationships, contracted alliances, and profit margins are the norm, leaving the high incidence of violence that marked the end of the last century as a nasty memory. This new era of professional business makes the TCOs far more dangerous and far more powerful than any other threat faced by law enforcement.

Transnational organised crime groups and multi-national corporations share a number of common characteristics – by design rather than coincidence. Both continually strive for increased professionalism and efficiency in their operations, with a dedication that cannot be matched by their less-organised brethren. They also have proven highly adept at implementing expansionist policies to gain larger shares of existing markets, regardless of competition. While the products and services vary greatly, the degree of influence that they wield often rivals or even surpasses that of small countries. That is as true of the Yakuza as it is of Microsoft. And as the TCOs get ever more powerful – some multinationals appear to be becoming more ruthless.

Both multinationals and TCOs rose to their current positions through a combination of ruthlessness and solid business savvy. Both groups have run the gauntlet of rivals, difficulties in management and resource allocation, and the problems associated with expansion. As such, they have managed to hone their operations to a level of efficiency that is both largely unnecessary and simply beyond the capability of groups restricted to national level operations. Both exhibit strong command structures, defined policies, and the ability to survive in the hostile political environments of other cultures.

Both groups have also accumulated enough power and influence to allow them effectively to exist outside of national boundaries. This grants them great flexibility in their operations, and provides them with a level of immunity that is impossible when one's assets are based in a given geographic location. Showing little regard for any nation's laws or boundaries, their enterprises often span entire continents. Thanks to the wonders of modern technology, a group's entire capital can be shifted from one end of the Earth to the other in moments – there's no way the law can keep up. In the case of larger syndicates that have control of all aspects of an illicit network, they have proved impossible to stop. The best that a nation can hope for is simply to blunt their influence. As such, prosecutions against their members may shatter cells or small networks, but the parent organisation remains untouched. Of more concern is the fact that many of these organisations reap a yearly gross profit that far outstrips the budget of many countries. With such financial power, their reach and influence should not be overestimated.

Like most multinational corporations, the TCOs often maintain limited ties to their country of origin. This may be little more than surface-level interest, though, since little emphasis is placed upon anything resembling nationalism or any real long-term concern for the populace. The crime syndicates often offer employment to the people, soon becoming the basis for much of the local economy. For example, in 1999, Romanian Interior Minister Constantin Ionescu admitted that the black market, organised by criminal gangs, accounts for as much as 40 per cent of the country's economy.

While the TCOs are provided with cheap labour and direct control over resources, they also gain the protection of a well-disposed community. Much like an insidious cancer, their presence cannot be cut out without inducing massive destabilisation across entire regions. Like the multinationals, the crime syndicate often proudly promotes its association to a country of origin, even influencing the organisational identity and name. The syndicates often extend the association to dictate the ethnicity of members that can hold power, which multinationals may not – officially, at least.

Not all multinationals place as much emphasis upon loyalty as the TCOs. One exception is the Japanese *zaibatsu* mega-corporations, where absolute loyalty is expected to the parent organisation and fellow staff in preference to one's own needs or interests. Significant resources are directed to cultivate internal loyalty, to guarantee cohesion and ensure survival.

Finally, one interesting comparison between the multinationals and transnational organised crime groups regards their methods of operations. Overall, overt violence for nearly any purpose is regarded with a particular type of distaste. Having learned that violent conflict is often far more costly than is acceptable – both in terms of organisational stability and profit – both groups are known to go to significant lengths to avert it. Of course, bloodshed sometimes represents the last available option to a TCO, when more civilised methods like negotiation cannot provide an acceptable end.

While this process is officially frowned upon by most legitimate corporations, documented events show that both multinationals and organised crime groups show no compunction about engaging in less than honourable tactics – including assassination, terrorism, and even government coups – to advance their interests. For example, a Canadian oil giant is facing a $1 billion class action lawsuit from a US anti-slavery group that alleges it has connived in ethnic cleansing in southern Sudan. Three leading soft drinks companies in Colombia face accusations in a Florida court of complicity in the murder of union leaders.

When violence is approved by the TCO, it is generally used as surgically as possible – as in the assassination of key individuals such as government officials, judges, and military leaders that are obstacles to the organisation's enterprises. As often as not, the killings are used to promote (or protest) policies and persuade unwilling opponents to concede. Examples from recent years in

South America illustrate this capability quite clearly. According to Amnesty International, Guatemalan businessman Edgar Ordóñez Porta, who died in 1999, was probably murdered after he started a small oil-refining business with his brother Hugo. The Ordóñez refinery is thought to have been seen as a threat to the vested interests of a group of military officers complicit in a 'corporate mafia state' – one in which companies, authorities and criminals collude to maintain their own economic interests.

At other times, more extreme examples of violence are required in order to gain the desired results, and the true influence of the syndicates becomes evident. Staying in Guatemala, Amnesty also claims that a series of bloody massacres in a village called Río Negro in 1980–82 could have been related to the construction on village land of a hydroelectric power plant in which the military had a stake. In the past, this has included the instigation of civil unrest and the complete destabilisation of entire regions within countries of the third world. The level of violence used depends upon the interests of the syndicate responsible. If it is simply making a relatively small move such as attempting to persuade a rival group to back down, the troubles will cease far more readily than if the goal is to inflict serious injury to a rival organisation as a whole. The Colombian drug war of the late 1980s is a good case in point. With the resources that the TCOs now have available, their capabilities have proven nearly limitless.

The TCOs are woven throughout our societies, tied in so closely that they are impossible to see. Collectively, they have more money and elite soldiers at their disposal than any western nation. If they wanted atomic bombs and fighter jets, they would simply steal them. Their intelligence networks equal those of any domestic

security group. They are utterly ruthless, without com-
passion, and interested only in controlling their markets
and squeezing as much profit as possible out of the
world. The only rules they play by are their own. If they
wanted to take over, it would be almost impossible to
stop them – and they continue to become more united,
more professional, and more dangerous. The new world
order is a criminal reality.

5. THIS ISLAND BRITAIN

THE FIRMS

The traditional image of British criminals is that of a smooth-talking 'geezer' selling bootleg tobacco out the back of the van at a car boot sale, or of a tracksuit-wearing kid with a crowbar and a torch shinning up a drainpipe to nick someone's DVD player. Organised crime in Britain has done an excellent job of hiding in the shadows. Instead, the media draws attention to the small-time crooks, the independent dealers who present about as much of a personal threat to the country as the average sewer rat.

The true situation is far more structured than most people would care to believe. Well-organised gangs, known as firms, have handled organised crime in all the major cities for a long time. These firms have a long-standing tradition to uphold, and each one of them specialises in a particular type of crime, being careful (for the most part) not to encroach on to other gangs' territory.

Organised crime entered its modern incarnation in Britain during the late 1950s and early 1960s, and the first big names of that era were the Kray Brothers. The Krays did something that no other firm had ever done – they brought the various feuding criminal families together and shared out the illegal activity in London so that no one would fight over the pieces. They kept the largest share for themselves, but they made sure that all the other firms had enough to keep them going. This was backed up with extreme action against any group stepping out of line. In this manner, they preserved a fragile peace between the families. When the Krays were finally brought to justice, the bonds that kept the firms together went with them, and the enforced truce collapsed. The various gangs quickly fell back to fighting among themselves.

In the majority of cases, the firms make an effort to maintain a façade of respectability. This is all the public generally sees. Many firms operate a number of entirely legitimate businesses as cover. Unlike most criminal fronts, these operations are kept strictly legitimate, without engaging in illegal practices or being used to launder money. This is unusual since most organised criminal groups find the convenience of front companies too tempting to resist, and the businesses quickly become compromised, but the British firms have a strong tradition of keeping their fronts as legitimate as possible. They will employ regular staff in perfectly honest positions – people who have no idea about the true nature of their employers, and who, if asked, will honestly answer that they don't know of any illegal goings-on within their premises or of any links between the boss and criminal groups. These innocents provide an invaluable cover for the hardened criminals hiding behind them.

The true nature of the firms is their street face, and few people ever get to see this – even in the criminal fraternity. The street face is not a pleasant one; it stays out of sight as much as possible, and acts swiftly and brutally, to minimise exposure. Anything is possible when you keep out of sight, because what the law doesn't see, the police can't get involved with. Even leaving the obvious matter of public interest aside, if the public facade were all that was ever seen by anyone, the firms would be a lot happier for it.

To make the most of the cover value of their fronts, firms generally choose business types that have little to do with the areas that are traditionally associated with criminal activity or corruption. This means that while almost all firms indulge to a greater or lesser degree in smuggling liquor and cigarettes into the country, they very rarely involve themselves in legitimate businesses associated with import of these goods. The link might give the police an extra reason to be suspicious or open investigations – and even if the risk is small, the British firms have reached their dominance by being careful.

Each firm is made up of fairly self-contained layers that employ a number of people. Exact numbers vary depending on the size and power of the firm, but in a big firm a single layer can be hundreds strong.

The lowest level in a firm is the home of the runners. These are usually young men and women, as yet untried and untested, who are trying to impress their masters. The goal is to be trusted with greater responsibility than the runner is currently being given. These people fall beneath the notice of both their employers and the police. There is nothing to be gained by taking one of these people into custody. They know nothing and are thought of as being worth nothing by their employer, so the costs and risks involved in apprehending them aren't worth the results. The only time that the runners acquire any sort of importance is when they can be traced back to the people above them, who in turn might provide a link to someone who does know something – or when the police have an arrest quota to be filled.

The level above the runners is the movers. These criminals control the day-to-day activities of the firm. They deal with the runners and set the assignments. If there is any breach of security, this is as far as the trail will lead, unless the authorities have managed to buy themselves a higher-level contact. Each mover is given an area to control, and all things within that area are their responsibility. They are left pretty much to their own devices by their immediate superiors. This may seem like a good deal for the movers, but they are also responsible if anything goes missing within their area, or if anything untoward happens. The movers have by far the most dangerous position, neither low enough to escape the attention of the authorities, nor high enough to have the power to do anything about it. They bide their time and try to survive until they can move up to the next level.

The movers report to the bosses. Different organisations have different names for these people, but they all amount to much the same thing. A boss is not The Boss; he or she is effectively a lieutenant, someone to deal with the issues that superiors can't be bothered with, and to provide a further layer of insulation from the authorities. In business terms, the bosses are middle management – accountable for the actions of the people beneath them, but without the true power of the board of directors. The bosses control districts rather than merely towns or shops, and all the information from their region will be passed to them before it gets to the top.

The head of the firm is usually from one of the major crime families. These individuals are high-level operators. They will never get directly involved in daily business affairs, controlling matters from a safe distance through intermediaries. About the only people who will get to meet with them are other criminals of a similar stature. The head will have hundreds, sometimes thousands, of people working for him, but will always personally conduct business in a manner that cannot incriminate him should anything go wrong. The only time that these people might ever become visible is if there is a major operation going on – one that the authorities already have some sort of lead on. Even when someone of this level is out and about, the authorities have to be careful – as the head of a firm will have teams of lawyers standing by to save him from any accusations that are levelled directly at him.

Few people in the law enforcement and criminal communities will ever see the head of a firm. Generally, the highest person who maintains any sort of presence on the street will be a boss, and even then he or she will be a rare sight. No career criminal likes being in the spotlight, even after retirement. Despite the number of personal exposés you can find on the bookshelves, almost anyone involved in serious organised crime stays well out of the way. The stories and events described in that sort of book or article are always already public knowledge, and they're hedged around with a lot of words like 'possibly', 'allegedly' and 'maybe'. Giving out hard facts is dangerous for an insider, and no one wants to do it. The reasons are simple. If you expose another criminal, the retaliation will be savage, and on top of that a statute of limitation does not bind many crimes, and if you write about something serious you have done but which wasn't previously known about, the police will investigate. No matter how much a criminal celebrity wannabe wants a book to sell, it's not worth taking the risk.

There are a few examples of people who have been on the wrong side of the law finding fame and fortune by telling all. In almost every case however, that person is trading on the romantic 'rough diamond' image – they may have been men of violence, but they were also men of honour. To be fair, a number of the people who managed to make the transition from villain to celebrity ex-criminal, maintained a code that they lived by. Men like Lenny 'the Guvnor' McLean and Roy 'Pretty Boy' Shaw were violent, but public record shows that they did follow standards of a sort. This was a feasible option during the times that they were active. However, today's British criminals are violent and unpredictable, and they live by the code of 'everything I can grab is mine'. These people are vicious and unprincipled in every way, and they are the ones who make up the majority of the modern firms.

Reports of muggings, burglaries, vicious assaults and other criminal activities flood British newspapers every day – so much so that the police are now investigating just one third of all street robberies in many areas. These crimes appear to be random, unconnected events – and perhaps a small number of them are. However, as the tide of crime continues to rise, some patterns become visible. Many of the crimes committed every day are not in the least bit random or accidental. One example was the brutal assault of a businessman in central London late in 2001. He was assaulted leaving the underground station at Mile End, and severely injured. His wallet was taken, and he was left in an alleyway. However, his mobile phone, his portable computer and his briefcase were all left alone. The police report indicated that they suspected gang involvement, as nothing to do with his business had been damaged or taken. Authorities surmised that the victim himself had some connection with one of the London firms, but without the active co-operation of the man, nothing could be done to take the matter further. Hiding punishment assaults, contract slayings and gang wars within the general pool of random muggings, rapes, murders and disappearances is one of the favourite tricks of the British firms. Terror is a potent weapon, and they make full use of it.

BUSINESS AS USUAL

Nightclubs are a favourite cover business for UK firms. Firm-owned clubs are a staging post and sales ground for all sorts of activities – from prostitution and drug dealing through to organisation and recruitment within the firm. Although nightclubs are checked on a regular basis by the enforcement agencies, for the most part the police don't have the time or the manpower to conduct regular searches. They tend to rely on the clubs' owners to contain any problems. This system works well most of the time, but it does mean that clubs which are owned by one of the firms become a perfect cover for all manner of criminal scheming.

The only time that crime in one of these nightclubs reaches public awareness is if one of the clubbers reports it, which rarely happens. The most common crimes within these places involve drug dealing and other substance trafficking. This is not the small-scale 'D'ya wanna buy an E, mate?' dealing that goes on in just about every nightclub worldwide. In firm-run nightclubs, the stakes are much higher. All that is required is a word – and it can be any innocuous word – but saying the word to the right person is the only way of establishing identity. Once that is taken care of, whatever the firm has to offer is available, in the sorts of quantities that make headline news at Dover. Firms will only allow their own products to be sold within their nightclubs, so that they can control any independent stupid enough to try to get some of the action.

Nightclubs of this sort maintain unusually heavy surveillance, both inside and outside the premises. Unlike regular security surveillance systems, this is not used to detect people doing illegal things, but rather to give the club owners warnings when there are problems of a legal nature. When the police raid a building, they can't just send in one man as they do in the films; they have to go in force. Anything less would be lethal. Large groups of police approaching are a sight that all staff are trained to look out for. Club owners may only get half a minute's warning before the police come through the door, but that's usually enough time to stash most of the drugs. The firms traditionally leave a small amount of product around for the police to find, as there usually is in regular nightclubs. Finding absolutely no trace of any wrongdoing would be suspicious.

Firms that operate clubs are careful about how they run them, as anything that goes on in the club can usually be traced back to the owners. If the owners have their fingers in more pies than just the club, then there is every possibility that the link will be found and acted upon. Consequently, clubs are usually set up in the name of one particular little-known mover, whose role might be just to manage the operation there.

In some clubs – particularly those in and around London – more than just drugs are available. Some clubs offer firearms, and can act as armouries for the firms that frequent and own them. In places like this, the entire staff of the club will be in on the enterprise because of the risk that an honest person might go directly to the police. Consequently, the firms use runners to crew clubs like this – and sometimes even to act as punters, too.

This means that police trying to gather evidence have to resort to undercover work within the club, trying to get enough data to make something out of it. This is very dangerous and extremely difficult, as the firms have a whole network of professionals who make absolutely sure that no one getting involved with the firm is any more than they say. With a huge pool of established and well-known runners to draw from, the firms are rightly very wary of using anyone outside the group for sensitive positions – and runners who seem too eager to get work in a club may be quietly disposed of just in case.

The firms are up to far more than just smuggling drugs and weapons through dodgy nightclubs, though. Armed robbery is a favourite activity of some despite the fact that it's a high stakes business. The profits are huge – often millions of pounds – but, if caught and convicted, the criminal is looking at a long stretch in the jail, usually a minimum of ten years, but optionally as many as 25.

Only the people who have the finance and the connections to put together a team and equip it can attempt this type of crime. Of the 4,000 plus armed robberies that took place in and around London during 2001, over 700 have been tentatively linked to just one firm. The gangs that were captured and brought to justice belonged mostly to the smallest and least-organised firms.

Firms that have been in the game for quite some time know who to hit and how to hit them. Financial institutions, particularly banks and building societies, are the usual. Planning a job of this sort takes time – lots of time if it is going to be done correctly – and large robberies can't be attempted too often in one firm's territory without the authorities coming down hard. As a result, no area is turned over more than once a year by the firms unless the security procedures at a given place are too invitingly lax.

Most firms practise some kind of extortion racket. They threaten people with violence unless they hand over cash or some kind of favour or service. It first became a common practice in the UK at the beginning of the early 1950s, and it has never gone out of fashion.

Protection money was levied on businesses that couldn't protect themselves. Firms that took care of the protection racket were careful not to arouse the suspicions of the police.

Firms getting established in extortion generally operate by making an example of one particular business, as an object lesson to the others that they are attempting to coerce. Usually this takes the form of entirely burning down that business's premises at night, once the staff has left. The business gets to claim on insurance, which allows it to start again, but it leads to massive inconvenience and loss of profits while the insurance process drags on. Most businesses simply move out of the area before starting up again. Warnings of this sort serve two purposes – firstly, they establish that the firm is willing to do what it is threatening to do, and secondly, that there is no lenience for any defaulters. By avoiding personally injuring or killing anyone, the firm also slashes the level of police interest, maintaining their security.

When the habit of extorting money from businesses was first starting, the police and the other authorities tried to suppress it by setting up regular patrols that kept threatened businesses under surveillance. This might have worked, if they had been dealing with an ordinary threat. However, the firms just switched tactics, and instead of threatening the business directly, they threatened the owners and their families and staff. After the first few defaulters found members of their families badly beaten or worse, they stopped going to the police. The firms had the first victory of the war, and extortion was quickly established as a regular source of reliable income.

Blackmail is no longer used as widely as it once was. Either people are more careful or the world is less shockable. It has become far more difficult for firms to dig up things that will be damaging enough to make people want to protect them. This does not mean that they don't do it anymore, but it does mean that with the extra work that it requires, only the largest firms take that sort of work on. They are the only ones with the manpower to do the digging, and follow up on the leads that they get to see if they can yield anything usable. For the most part, blackmail is now a crime of opportunity. There are legions of petty underworld informers who occasionally hear things. When they do, most of the time, these informants will freely volunteer any information they have just to appear useful to the firm that they are reporting to – anything that will increase their standing with the firm. Usable information is generally rewarded, and useful informers may be taken on as runners, getting a foothold in the firm. The right kind of scandal can still be enough to ruin certain careers.

Assassination is another firm speciality. There is always plenty of work for an enterprising killer. The absolute rule in these matters is that while the firms arrange all the killings, they will never let any of their own people take care of the execution. Instead, there is a hard core of independent operators who deal with terminations.

Arranging a death is easy for those who know the trade – the only thing that really complicates matters is whether the purchaser wants the death to appear accidental or if they want it to be clear that the person in question was murdered. In most cases, they prefer the death to look accidental. The usual method of faking an accidental death is by staging a car crash or some similar event, such as drowning or a gas explosion at home – anything that leaves no obvious reason to suspect how the person died. If the victim is not famous, high-profile, a high security risk or important in the criminal world, then a simple 'botched mugging' or 'tragically fatal street violence' execution costs as little as £2,000.

One type of crime that has taken the firms' fancy recently is carjacking. The standard *modus operandi* when carjacking is for a gang of men to cruise around in two vans looking for targets. Several of them will be armed with hand weapons, such as crowbars, cudgels and, occasionally, swords and knives. They drive around areas where exclusive and expensive cars are to be found and wait till they find one that looks like it will be worth the effort. If the risk of the carjacking is outweighed by the profit to be gained by selling the vehicle or the goods within it, they proceed.

If the car itself is going to be stolen, the criminals wait until it is in a relatively isolated position, hidden from street-side cameras and with no easy exits. The first van blocks the road in front of the car, while the second one boxes it in from behind. Once the target car is immobilised, the criminals in the vans get out and smash their way into the vehicle, drag out the occupants – and attack them if necessary – then take the car, along with any other valuables that might be available.

In 2002 a young businesswoman found herself followed to her house in Kensington while she was driving home one night. When she attempted to get from her vehicle and into her home, she was attacked by five armed men who badly injured her and left her in her driveway. Because of the time of night that the attack took place, the police took 15 minutes to get to her, and this was only because one of her neighbours was locking up the house and noticed her lying in the street.

Not everyone gets away quite so lightly. Late in 2001, a middle-aged couple were returning to their house in the country from a night at the opera in London when they were attacked and robbed by a gang of six men. The woman survived the assault, and later testified to the police that the robbers had known what they were carrying and where they were going. The attack took just four minutes and, at the end of it, her husband was dead and their car and possessions stolen. Piecing together the movements of the couple, the police later guessed that the gang had seen the couple leaving the opera and had originally decided to rob them of the Rolex watches they had been wearing. The gang then upgraded the plan when they realised that the couple were driving an Aston Martin DB7 – a very expensive and exclusive car. The gang followed them to a deserted road in the middle of the countryside and then made their move, forcing the car off the road. The woman was found by a police car that happened to be going past on routine patrol.

The major problem with trying to combat carjacking is that the crime is extremely fast. The criminals are constantly on the move. By the time the crime is reported – and any professional criminal knows how fast (or slowly) the police take to respond – the perpetrators are long gone. The gangs know which areas are the most stretched for police resources and, where possible, will strike there.

The locations that are the best for full carjacking tend to be the worst for in-car theft, and vice versa, so every location offers opportunities. Very few carjackings take place in central London, for several reasons. The police patrol the area regularly, almost all of central London is observed by close-circuit television, and the roads are perpetually in a state of near gridlock. It's perfect for in-car theft, though. The quiet backstreets of Kensington, for example, are full of expensive cars. Some car manufacturers are coming up with new ways to try to combat the carjacking problem – such as Rhino Glass windows, which can withstand £2,000 per square inch impact without damage – but as long as there are expensive cars, carjacking will remain a problem.

A less violent but highly profitable sideline for almost all firms is bootlegging. The criminals go to markets, fairs or car boot sales and sell fake items that appear to be genuine or original, or that do the same job. This is a lucrative activity as the fines charged by the police are minimal while the returns that are available can be astronomical. The stereotypical examples are the pirate videos and compact discs that can be found being openly sold in most markets and boot sales. These videos can be produced by anyone with two VCR machines and one simple wire – although most pirates use professional duplication systems that can write a dozen films at a time – just as CDs can be copied by anyone with a computer and a CD-ROM writer. The whole process takes mere minutes, and takes only the tiniest hint of technical knowledge. When you factor in the cost of the blank videos and CDs, which can be bought in bulk at very low prices, the criminals net between five and ten pounds per copy, for an outlay of something like 50p.

Another form of bootlegging is the sale of contraband and illegally smuggled goods from abroad. The most common are cigarettes and alcohol, which can be acquired cheaply overseas and brought back to Britain for little cost providing that the Customs officers do not find you. Stacks of contraband can be found at Sunday markets of all types, frequently sold by illegal immigrants recruited for the purpose by the firms. The police periodically raid these markets, usually in force and with backup from various other agencies, but there is little that they can do to the people selling the goods. The criminals are fully aware of this – it's the reason they prefer using foreigners. Many of the immigrants cannot even speak English, having been taught just enough to explain that they are refugees when they are apprehended. If the person is eventually deported rather than given asylum, it is no loss for the criminals.

Where possible, firms generally pay cash in hand. It may not seem particularly serious, but by paying people cash in hand, the criminals are not only taking tax money from the state, they are also giving it to people who are probably claiming benefits in the first place. It places a double burden upon the taxpayer. As a result, the government has to raise taxes to pay for the essentials of state welfare, and it is the taxpayers who suffer.

Some analysts believe that the firms have recruited hundreds of people simply to work over the British benefits system. Some firms specialise in acquiring National Insurance numbers. This may not seem to be a great fraud either, until you realise that with a National Insurance number, you gain most of the rights and privileges of any British citizen, including the right to benefit and free care from the state. The firms assemble thousands of these numbers, and then use them to fraudulently obtain tens of thousands of pounds every week in benefits. Common practice is to have the money paid straight into a dedicated holding account.

Some of the firms even employ people just to sign on at different agencies across a district. Each person will usually sign on no more than once in each town, so that there is little risk of being recognised. With enough National Insurance numbers, one person can sign on twenty or more times a week, netting up to quarter of a million for the firm a year between unemployment benefit and housing benefit.

ORGANISATIONS

There are several firms that operate in the UK, and each of the larger groups has control over a portion of the country. We cannot name the major players, because the evidence to support that sort of allegation is impossible to obtain, and legal teams would recommend that this kind of information should not get published. However, there are a number of groups whose activities are a matter of public record.

According to one seasoned observer of the UK organised crime scene, one particular family has sewn up Newcastle. The gang includes over 100 people, ranging from accountants down to street muscle. They are said to control all the prostitution and car crime in the area, and are responsible for most of the criminal activity that goes on there. They normally have several gangs patrolling the streets, both in cars and on foot. These gangs will be on one of two different jobs. One duty is to follow the firm's prostitutes and make sure that nothing untoward happens to them. This is not done out of any concern for the woman in question, but rather with an eye to protecting the value of the firm's investment. The other standard duty involves prowling the city, looking for opportunities to steal or hijack cars, mug wealthy individuals, and so on.

Apparently, this particular firm likes to combine activities. For example, if one of the prostitutes is entertaining a likely looking client, the gang watching her will head over to the prostitute, then rob and batter the punter, leaving him for dead. When he recovers, the combination of shock and the shame of admitting the circumstances is usually enough to make sure that the victim does not report the theft and injury. In addition some of the victims have been so desperate to keep the details from their families that they have been prepared to pay continuing blackmail sums in order to keep it all quiet. The firm has been caught on a couple of cases where the victims decided they didn't mind speaking out after all, and several members of the firm were sent down to serve their time. That said, in both the cases, all the information on the victim was released to the police and through them to the courts and the press. In both instances, the victim found himself on the edge of professional and personal ruin.

In London, another family allegedly controls a good part of the slave trade. It may seem astonishing that the UK still has an active slave trade, but like all things criminal, the brightest lights cast the darkest shadows – and London does have such very bright lights. The firms know that most people cannot believe that slavery is still going on in Britain, and that in itself is one of the most powerful shields that any criminal can have. Apparently, this firm has invested a lot of money in this slick operation. People are rumoured to be brought in on private aircraft. This allows them to get people through the·gates with minimal paperwork and security checks, and costs a tiny fraction of the money that the slaves will bring in.

It is a simple business transaction; it costs no more than £5,000 (and often far less) to get a slave into Britain, and the victim's value is considerably higher. The cost of import will be recouped in wages alone early in the first year. The annual minimum wage in Britain is around £4 an hour which means that just using a slave as an unpaid employee, the firm makes its money back within a matter of months. And that's not making any allowances for the hours that slaves are forced to work. Multiply the annual wage saving by the number of years that the slave will work before being killed – which varies from person to person – and the total profit is vast. Sale value of a slave is a proportion of their expected lifetime worth. Slaves who are being used in the sex industry, or who are being sold to private 'collectors' as personal toys, will fetch an even higher price, particularly pretty young females.

This total disdain for human suffering is reflected in all the firms' practices. Smuggled refugees are typically used as drugs carriers, so that when they are brought over, they carry enough cargo to make up the cost of getting them there in the first place. Examples of this are common. A woman was arrested at Heathrow in 1995 having been brought over on a commercial aircraft. All her papers were in order and she was travelling first class. There would have been no reason to take any notice of her, except that she collapsed on her way through the terminal and had to be rushed to the first aid station. She turned out to be suffering from a massive heroin overdose.

The police were called, and while they were en route, the woman took a turn for the worse. She was X-rayed on one of the devices at Heathrow, and the medical staff found that her abdominal cavity was holding an artificial device. The authorities were given emergency authorisation to save the woman's life, and they operated at the medical facility at Heathrow. Thirteen kilogrammes of heroin were retrieved from her abdomen.

The firm that brought her over was never found, but under direct questioning, the woman indicated that they had been preparing her for several months to act as a drugs carrier. They had filled her abdomen with drugs before sending her over, and had been holding several of her family members hostage to make sure that she behaved herself. The firm had been planning to use her and a number of similar women as carriers for their drugs, knowing that the sheer volume of drugs that each woman could carry was more than enough to cover the costs and risks associated.

In this instance, the gang had not accounted for the risk that the flight might be delayed – as it in fact was. With the extra wait, the woman's stomach acids had eaten through the walls of one of the bags of drugs that she was carrying inside her. Her system was massively flooded with heroin, which caused her to collapse. If the firm that had employed her had considered that possibility, there wouldn't have been any problem in the first place. She would probably still be being forced to carry drugs.

This sort of use of drugs 'mules' is an important part of the narcotics smuggling process. It makes the firms a lot of money, and was the speciality of another eminent UK criminal clan. This firm specialised in smuggling refugees into the country and loading them up with drugs beforehand. They were even said to have used corpses to transport the drugs. They would hire corrupt medical personnel to take bodies of deceased British subjects from the morgue, split them open and fill them with narcotics, then sew them back up and send them over to be buried in their home country.

In many instances, the relatives of the deceased were in on the deal, and had been paid off by the firm in exchange for their silence, and for the violation of their loved one. The payoff on several kilogrammes of class A narcotics can be in the hundreds of thousands – even millions, if it is cut with other substances – so the tiny payoff that they gave to the bereaved barely touched the profits.

This firm was closed down when undercover operatives from various branches of Interpol teamed up with police forces on both sides of the world to take care of the problem once and for all. The case itself was open and shut, and attracted little publicity. Details of the police operation were not broadcast at the time in the hope that the bigger firms that had been working with them would continue using the same method to bring the drugs in, and so be exposed.

FOREIGN VISITORS

For a long time the firms had no problems with external groups, as the British crime scene was tightly sewn up. No one got in without first going through the firms, and no groups tried to muscle in as the entire scene was under such tight control. This started changing when the first of the visiting gangs got a foot in the door. Even though all the members of the criminal world want to be the king of the heap, they're not above using other people to get what they want. This creates opportunities, as every criminal organisation has something to offer the others.

The first visitors to establish a beachhead in Britain were the Jamaican Yardies, and they brought their culture and crime history with them. This included gunrunning on a grand scale, and their own particular ways of dealing drugs. Life is cheap for all organised criminals, but the Yardies were particularly casual about killing.

Guns are an everyday fact of life in much of Jamaica, as is the violence that they breed. Many of the Yardie gangs are thought to have links to international shipping and freight companies which they use to transport huge cargo containers loaded to the brim with illegal weaponry for sale on our streets. In most of the major cities in Britain, it is quite easy to obtain an illegal firearm within an hour if you have the money and the connections. In many cases, just the money will do, as these people really don't care to whom they sell. A survey taken in 1998 by the *News of the World* newspaper listed weapons acquired by their reporters during a week on the streets. The haul included three fully automatic rifles, 14 handguns, 37 knives, and assorted other weapons, including compressed-air tasers. The reporters had gone into London's Soho area, spent time in some of the bars there, and had quickly been given names and contact details of people who could supply them with weapons. They simply had to hand over the money to complete the transaction.

The problem, the paper said, was not that the weapons were available, but that the people who deal in them were easy to contact without being easy to trace. Usually the Yardies use a runner to make all the initial contacts, leaving no lead back to themselves. Once the contact is verified as a 'legitimate' deal, they will hand over the weapons but take the address of the client in question. This is mainly so that if something goes wrong, the Yardies know where to go to get revenge, but also so that they can keep an eye on the client's future needs. The reporters involved in the case had to move homes – even though they had not given real addresses to the Yardies – and start again elsewhere because of the threats and violence that they were suffering.

After the Yardies were established in Britain in the 1980s, other groups started to make their way in. The Russians were quick to arrive, and had established a significant presence by the early 1990s. Since the dissolution of the Soviet Union, a lot of regional warlords have taken power in their own provinces. In many cases, the heads of certain regions also had access to the military equipment that their region was using at the time. In almost every case, they were willing to sell the weapons to anyone who could pay for them. This has led to a great amount of weaponry coming over, both as smuggled arms, and as the working tools of Russian mobsters. The other resource that the Russians have great amounts of is human labour, particularly prostitution. The Soviet Union was an immense country geographically, and outside the major cities the population is spread out thinly. This has led to an alarming increase in the number of people who disappear in Russia every year.

Russian law enforcement is still weak, recovering from the transition to democracy and the years of anarchy and disruption that followed. Consequently, Russian organised crime has almost total contempt for the law and the Organizatsiya is unsubtle to say the least. This as much as anything else has helped stop them gaining an even greater presence in Britain than they currently have. The UK firms do not want anyone messing up their territory – least of all the Russians, who deal with matters in one language only, force. It is not that the English firms fear the Russians, it is merely that the English criminal scene still relies on stealth, and the Russians are open about their extreme violence. The British firms see them as being simply too much hassle to have to deal with on a regular basis.

In contrast to the Russians, Asian gangs understand the subtleties of working in a state with active law enforcement. Chinese and Japanese organised criminals work in highly populated environments, and there are several areas that they can operate in with relative impunity. One of their major imports to the UK is people – given the size of the population there, human labour is cheap. A lot of illegal immigrants are brought over from Asia, either semi-voluntarily, to work for sweatshop rates for traditionally oriental businesses – catering, cleaning, laundry, clothes manufacture and so on – or involuntarily, for the sex and slave trades.

Unwanted girl children, the victims of China's strict 'one family, one child' policy, make up a significant number of these unfortunate people.

A greater Oriental threat comes from designer drugs. Drug lords set up their own chemical plants and produce their own drugs in South East Asia. They test these drugs on the endless client base that they have in their own countries and, when they are satisfied with the results, they export them.

The final trade from the East is technology. The development and production costs of technology are driven down by the sheer volume of people who can work on a project. Technology doesn't have an inherent client base, however, and it is not addictive in the same way that narcotics are. The people buying technology usually have a purpose for it and, as such, will not need to do much repeat buying. There are stories of hundreds of thousands of personal stereos, car stereos, and other small items found in a single container by Customs. The street value of these items is low and, in many cases, such containers are left behind as decoys to distract the authorities from the drug smuggling that is going on. A freight container full of compact disc players might fetch £100,000, while a freight container full of designer drugs will easily bring in upwards of £10 million.

Smuggled goods from the Far East often come in by sea. This is because piracy is another speciality of certain Far Eastern TCOs. When they want to take care of transporting equipment and goods from one country to another, they often simply commandeer a vessel and carry them over personally, thus eliminating the need to pay off those who are already on the ship.

Cultural attitudes have kept the Far Eastern gangs relatively quiet in the United Kingdom. The crimes they prefer are low profile, and the people who run the gangs are insular by nature. It is all simply business. So far, the Triads and Yakuza have been content to keep to their operations mostly within their ethnic communities, and pay due respect to the firms.

British firms appear to work in partnership with the Latin American drug cartels. The advantages for both sides are too good to mess up. The Latino drug lords are happy to stay on home soil and let the firms control UK distribution. The drugs cartels in Mexico and Colombia export their home-produced drugs to anyone world-wide, and they do so using the vast networks of people at their command. The Colombian cartels obtained a huge pool of labour by addicting entire towns and villages to their product, so that the people there work reliably and cheaply, taking part payment in kind. This provides the British firms with an endless supply of 'disposable' couriers. The average shipment of drugs from Latin America is now little more than a few kilos, but these small amounts can be sent with such regularity that they can quickly import several tons in almost perfect safety. If a courier is stopped, it's a mere fraction of the shipment, not the whole lot. The British firms then 'water down' the product that they get, making sure that their imports go even further and are more profitable. Even though the days of the Colombian drugs superstars are gone, the cartels remain very rich and very powerful. They could cause serious problems for the firms if they were expansionist, but they are content to stay at home in safety and rake in the billions.

The Albanians are a different matter entirely. They are hungry to expand. They have nothing left to lose, either, so they are extremely violent. Like the Russians, they lack subtlety, so they have yet to do really well in the UK, but they have a strong presence here, and they are getting bigger and stronger all the time. The Albanian gangs here engage in all forms of trafficking, street crime and fraud, and there may come a time when they seriously challenge the firms for power. They are already making life difficult for the Turkish and Pakistani drugs gangs in Britain who have been working with the firms for years.

As part of the Golden Crescent of major heroin-producing countries, Pakistani gangs have been a significant contributor to the drugs trade for decades. The current generation of Pakistani drug lords have even become a quasi-respectable part of Pakistani society, through various schemes that have allowed profits to be laundered. The drug money supports a significant underground economy – according to the Pakistan Institute of Development Economics, the black economy had grown in size from 20 per cent of GDP in 1973 to over 51 per cent in 1996. The Pakistani drugs gangs have worked with the Sri Lankan Tamil Tiger separatists over the last fifteen years, and now co-operate closely with them on weapons deals, drugs shipping issues and other smuggling requirements. The gangs use kinship links to merge into international Pakistani expatriate communities and operate in the UK and elsewhere without attracting undue notice.

The other organised criminal groups in Europe have little to do with the United Kingdom. There isn't much that they have to offer the firms, and so there are few dealings between them. German criminal groups usually deal in technology and guns – things that can be found far more easily further afield, and for a greater profit margin. The Italians are no longer the omnipresent force that they once were, and while the time-honoured Mafia activities of extortion, torture, and racketeering still go on, the British firms have been taking care of such matters themselves for decades, and don't have to go hiring in foreign muscle. In France, Spain and Benelux, the domestic criminal groups tend to deal in minor goods like lower-class drugs, and the Greeks are mainly independent petty fraudsters. While some of the small-time criminals in Britain have occasional dealings with the Europeans, the major firms hardly ever take an interest in anything on that scale. They prefer to stay where the profits are worth the risks.

When a foreign organisation deals with a British firm, a faction of the TCO based in the UK usually carries out business. Most of the major foreign organisations send smaller groups – sub-divisions, effectively – into Britain to make contact with the firms. When they do, the smaller groups are normally integrated into the British firm as part of the gang. Much like bridal exchanges in feudal Europe, this cements relationships between the two groups, and so gives each one a little more protection when dealing in the other's territory. It also gives both sides some leverage when dealing with the other – after all, it is far easier to negotiate when you have people within arm's reach. It also makes conducting business easier when the firm knows where their contacts live. If something goes wrong, both sides have someone to go to straight away.

The particularly secretive nature of organised crime in Britain has several implications. The firms are not really interested in international expansion. They only go out of the country when they need something that they cannot easily acquire domestically. When they do go out of the country, it is to follow an established link, so they know exactly where they are going. The firms keep a tight grip on their territories. This means that other organisations need their permission to operate. Get on the wrong side of one of the firms and the consequences are deadly. Like the Far Eastern clans, the British know that if they allow too much of their business to be taken over by outsiders, they run the risk of appearing weak – lethal for anyone in the criminal community.

This culture of isolation works both ways. It is harder for police and other authorities to penetrate the shells that the firms hide behind. At the same time, though, it is more difficult for the firms to take on new people without running the risk of opening themselves up to infiltration. It is a delicate balancing act for both sides of the law – and, at the moment, it's one that the firms are winning.

DOMESTIC CORRUPTION

Crime pays in hard cash, and nowadays, if you've got something that the firms want, it pays well. For many the temptation to take dirty money is too much to resist. Most firms have whole teams of professionals working on their behalf, usually people who are fully aware of all the things that are going on within their clients' businesses. After all, it doesn't take a brilliant accountant to realise that you don't spend several hundred thousand pounds on light fittings. Complicity brings its own risks with it, of course, and often the companies that do work for the firms are the ones that end up taking the hit for the criminals when they are finally caught.

Corruption takes many forms. The mildest is incidental corruption. From time to time, the firms will need a certain thing doing, or a service performed, which none of their own personnel can take care of. When a matter like this arises, the firm will approach a small company of professionals – usually one that is in financial difficulties or is having trouble in some other sector – and volunteer to help out, in return for a small bit of assistance in kind. Many small firms do not understand exactly what they are getting themselves into. By the time they realise what is going on, they are already in too deep to extricate themselves without causing themselves and their families some serious problems.

Once the firm has the company in its grasp, it will introduce more and more work for them to do, each time making sure that it is the company and not the firm which makes the relevant legal declarations. This serves two purposes – firstly, when the firm files its papers or documents, an official seal is administered to the paperwork; and secondly, should anything untoward happen, the firm can withdraw from the company that it has suborned and implicate them in the proceedings. All the paperwork will have been signed off by the company, and the firm will be able to show that they had no idea any impropriety had been taking place within their organisation. Many of the companies that are taken over in this way enjoy great success until the time comes for them to be sacrificed for the good of the firm.

Another common approach for the firms is the low-level corruption of police officers. Everyone knows what a 'bent copper' is. A police officer who is prepared to overlook certain events or botch arrests is a fantastic resource for any criminal organisation. Unfortunately given the average police officer's salary, there is every incentive to take a little bonus here and there, and practically no reward for those officers who do work above and beyond the call of duty.

Firms look out for police who have demonstrated a little sloppiness in their duty, and they keep a close eye on officers and patrol walkers who fit their profile. When they feel that the time is right, they will quietly send one of their people to make contact with the officer in question, indicating what it can be worth if they show a little leniency in the right place at the right time. The firm will always be happy to make all the payments that they promise, knowing that once the first few brown envelopes have been received, the officer who has been paid is compromised for good, and they will be able to ask for greater things from them. Former police officers have a particularly savage time of it in prison. With their usual caution, the firms will always make sure that there is no way that the officer can be connected to them – unless that would prove useful. If there is ever a need to 'out' the officer in question, then a few anonymous phone calls providing verifiable information to the right people can quickly destroy the officer's career.

Sometimes, the officer who is approached goes straight to his or her superiors with information about the offered bribe, and a counter-operation may take place to try to trap the firm. All too often, however, all that happens as a result of this sort of action is that the runner the firm sent out is implicated and caught, but by then the firm will have severed all links with that person, and will not approach the same officer again. Sadly, given the conditions that most police officers have to put up with, it is understandable that a very small minority of those officers who are approached give in to temptation and take the money. The hours are long, the work itself is hard and dangerous, and carried out on behalf of an often ungrateful public, with results that barely seem to scratch the surface of the criminal world.

Another form of low-level corruption is informing. The firms use informers in much the same way that the police do. The criminals are always looking for informers who work in positions that they can make use of. Typical examples include despatch managers for goods shipping operations, and people who hold keys and passwords for targets that the criminals want to raid. The right piece of information is worth far more than the effort required to get it, and all it takes is a few good informers to make a significant difference to a firm's income. The information that the firms most want to know usually involves the details of security systems in the areas that they are planning to rob. If they know where the security systems are and how to disable them, then the job can be done in half the time with half the people – well worth the small payoff that it takes to get the information.

Mid-level criminal corruption takes place within the business world. The basic belief on which the capitalist system is founded is that the person who offers the most attractive all-round deal will get the business. However, in reality, it is fairly common practice that the person who offers the most attractive personal incentive to the decision-maker will be the one who gets the business. This has several serious effects on the way that government and strategic economic policies end up working out – analysts tend to assume the core beliefs are true across the board.

There are several different ways that a bribe can be offered. Practically speaking, hard cash, property and shares in a business are always good bribes, but they can be very expensive in real terms. The most cost-effective bribes take the form of stolen goods that have been re-processed through the firm. The firm steals whatever the client wants, cleans it up and makes it look legal, then passes it on with their compliments in return for the business that they are after. In some cases, the goods are eventually tracked to their new owner and the authorities take back what was stolen. By that time, however, the firm will already have what they came for, and they will not be concerned with the outcome of any such case. They will have covered their tracks completely long before the bribe was ever handed over.

Another cheap method of bribing members of the business community is to offer information to people who can make use of it. This is done in several ways, and starts at the lower levels with information such as who is going to be tendering for relevant contracts when, and what they are likely to want to see from the successful bidder. This sort of knowledge can be worth hundreds of thousands of pounds to the right business. Higher levels of information bribery include inside information on stock markets, and brokering of data at a government level. This sort of information is only handed out by the largest and most important firms, and the money that can change hands is astronomical. When you consider that a single dead certainty on the stock market can be worth millions of pounds, any method of getting hold of that information is worthwhile. There are controls and industry standards in place to suppress this sort of thing, and the penalty for insider dealing can be severe. Naturally, the firm will always make sure that they themselves are not directly involved with the transaction.

6. GANGLAND AMERICA

STREET GANGS

Criminal gang activity within the United States has been known since the early nineteenth century, but current figures show that the problem has grown to epidemic levels. The street gangs feed off the interests of transnational organised crime, getting bigger, stronger and more organised. The TCOs in turn use the gangs as expendable manpower. With all parties profiting massively from the huge increase in illegal drug use during the 1980s, it is estimated that now over 30,000 individual street gangs exist across the country. Their total membership is thought to approach one million. Even though individual groups vary considerably in general disposition, ethnicity and influence, they are universally violent and involved in a range of criminal activities in their respective territories. Street gangs are a characteristic of the urban landscape of twenty-first century America and, given their tendencies for self-renewal and expansion, they are not going to vanish in the years to come.

Modern street gangs were first openly acknowledged as a serious threat to the fabric of society by law enforcement in the early 1970s, but little effective action was taken to counter them. It is unclear whether this was because police chiefs at the time thought that they did not have the potential to become a greater problem, or because sufficient resources to combat them simply were not available. Without any real controls stemming their expansion, the gangs were soon entrenched in nearly every urban area in the nation. Capitalising upon a variety of criminal enterprises, including drug trafficking and production, robbery, extortion, prostitution and contract murder, they have created their own step on the criminal ladder. They have also demonstrated influence over areas not normally considered open to low-level gangs – mainly elements within law enforcement, the military and the political arena.

Street gangs are generally less organised than other crime groups and frequently indulge in costly in-fighting that reduces their capabilities. During the 1970s and 1980s, clashes over territory, personnel and resources led to a high turnover in personnel and ensured that, to a certain extent, the gangs kept each other in check. Unfortunately, developments in recent years have shown that the streets are taking a lead from the TCOs, and getting smart and organised. Business interests have led to truces, co-operation and even mergers between gangs that had formerly been bitter rivals. Under the influence of international organised crime groups, the street gangs are shaping up to become more useful to the TCOs. These gang alliances look like becoming increasingly powerful in the future.

The basis for the modern street gang lies in the poverty and resentment rampant within America's urban sprawl. Street gangs represent the only achievable way out for many youths. In the ghetto, gang life can seem a sensible career choice. Without traditional support structures such as intact families, a decent education system or pastoral guidance, many youths find that they have few other options if they want to earn a living. Others see the wealth that the gangsters have, and look up to them as role models. Some find themselves in the same situation as those who arrived in America in the nineteenth century and had to band together to survive.

Gangs are consistently seeking new members, both to replace losses and to give them the manpower to expand their capabilities. A variety of techniques are employed, beginning subtly and gradually increasing in intensity. In many situations, the targeted recruit has no other option but to give in and join if he or she wants to stay alive.

The first step that is used to gain recruits is simple peer pressure. Potential recruits are approached by known gang members in friendly circumstances and asked to join. Many times, friends or relatives that the targets respect will be the ones who make first contact. The advantages of the gang – companionship, protection and status – are stressed. While this approach is normally friendly, the results can be quite intimidating because any who refuse know what will happen next.

The second step is harassment, and it is a long way from the friendly first contact. This time, gang members in colours approach and force a confrontation. Mild harassment and threats soon turn into assault, although the potential recruit will not usually be seriously injured. Further assaults occur no matter where the recruit goes, since the gang will be watching out for him or her. This level of harassment expands to include threats against family members and friends until the victim either submits, or the gang gets bored and decides to make an example of the victim.

The final step before the gang decides that the individual isn't adequate is an extension of the second stage. Someone that the target knows is badly injured or even killed as a warning, informing the target that this is their last chance to join. If the potential recruit refuses at this point, they will usually become the initiation test murder for the next upcoming recruit.

Street gangs are surprisingly well organised, and retain a ranking system for members based upon both merit and experience. The following ranking scheme is typical, and is taken from the system used by the Crips of Los Angeles. It ranges from mere associates to the hierarchy of the gang itself. The lowest level of gangland comprises associates who identify with and co-operate with the gang, perhaps as employees, but are not officially considered part of it. They are not subject to the same rules as actual members, but they need to remember the proper respect if they want to survive. A second level of gang associate is known as a peripheral, and refers to those who co-operate with the gang and receive perks such as protection. Peripherals maintain a friendly relationship with the gang in return for services such as being a 'mule' or managing a group of prostitutes. This rank also includes friendlies who are not officially connected to the group, but who take ordinary jobs in order provide information. The third type of associate is referred to as a 'gonna-be'. They work with the gang, actively seeking to be recruited to full membership. Gonna-bes frequently present themselves as gang members even though they are not, and they provide a recruitment pool for new members.

The actual first level within a gang is known as either a 'BG' for Baby Gangster or 'TG' for Tiny Gangster. These titles refer to younger members of the gang – often under the age of ten – who have not yet earned their position. Even at this age, BGs are learning the way the gang operates, and sometimes function as couriers or lookouts. They are usually considered too young for other duties, although they may be quite eager to try. During 1993, a fierce rivalry over drugs distribution erupted between two groups of TGs in Chicago. The head of one group, an eleven year old, was caught and arrested. He was executed a few days later in his cell by his ten-year-old rival, who had sneaked into the detention area with a pistol. The rival then tried to shoot his way out of the police station, and was killed.

The core of the gang, however, is composed of 'gangsters', the hardcore members and primary strength of the gang. Such individuals are extremely dangerous, may have served hard time, and will have a well-established reputation for crime. In many cases they are also responsible for the control of gang operations. Group leaders are known as 'OGs', which refers to either Original Gangster or Old Gangster, depending upon the group. These may be the founders of the group itself, or simply respected elders. They are sometimes referred to as 'shot callers', since they control the gang activities.

The gangs themselves are divided into sets or cliques, comprising a group of core members under a single leader – who may be an OG – directing their activities in certain assigned ventures. Several sets will operate under the control of a respected OG, similar to the way biker gang chapters operate. He or she may report to the equivalent of a 'regional director' in the primary gang. There is usually a single leader at the top in the case of smaller groups, or a committee in the case of gang alliances.

The most important aspects of gang life revolve around maintaining personal image, giving respect to superiors, and being loyal to the gang. This is often detailed in a code of conduct, along with penalties for violations that vary depending upon the gang and the culture it sprang from. Penalties range from beatings lasting for predetermined amounts of time, to torture, murder of loved ones and execution. Like the organised crime groups above them, the gangs rail against what they see as governmental oppression, but respond by imposing strict laws of their own with excessively severe punishments.

Gangs consistently use symbols, colours and graffiti as identifiers to mark both members and territory. While these vary widely, they are also commonly used for communication, to denote rank, and even to provide details of upcoming operations. The status of gang alliances and relations are also readily apparent from symbols like graffiti, and hostilities will often be telegraphed by a rash of corruptions of the rival group's chosen symbols.

Gang members generally possess fatalistic or hostile world views, but occasionally this may change when the individual realises that other lifestyles are possible. This is never a decision taken lightly, since the gang typically represents the only life that the person has known. Although the knowledge of what happens to those who turn traitor is a major disincentive, there are three known methods for getting out of a gang. Any member attempting them can expect to face severe resistance.

'Flipping' is the most hazardous of the options, and marks the gang member as an immediate traitor. Flipping entails discarding one's colours and gang markings, and joining a rival group. If the other group is not able or not willing to protect the turncoat, the new recruit can expect a painful demise at the hands of his former family and friends. Few gangs will allow a flipping member to survive.

In the case of the Latin Kings and a few other organisations, the only way to leave the gang short of dying is to convert fully to Christianity and request permission to retire. Provided that the member can prove that they are devout in their commitment – perhaps by accepting a potentially fatal beating as a test of faith – the leaders of the organisation will allow it.

The most difficult way for a member to break with their gang is to cut all connections and run. Much like a person in a witness protection program, the individual can never return to their former life again, and may need to flee to a different part of the country to survive the process. Regardless of their importance to the group, the gang will certainly try to locate them as a matter of honour.

One of the difficulties in legally addressing the problem of gangs has been the lack of clear definitions of what constitutes a gang, on both the state and federal levels. Since none exist, the effectiveness of anti-gang legislation has been greatly weakened. This has also prevented law enforcement agencies from being able to classify crimes as being gang-related, and distribute information accordingly. The following categories are from a new system created by the United States Department of Justice that classifies gangs into three proposed classes: Turf, Corporate and Scavenger.

TERRITORIAL OR TURF GANGS

The first type of gang is known as a territorial or turf gang. The primary purpose of a territorial gang is to gain control and influence within a particular urban area. These territories range in size from a section as small as the length of a street to one as large as an entire district of a city, depending upon the strength of the gang in question. In some cases, these gangs originally formed out of well-meaning unofficial neighbourhood-watch-style schemes for local self-defence. Unfortunately, once a degree of control and influence is established, these organisations expanded their operations into criminal activities such as racketeering and extortion in the neighbourhoods that they originally claimed to protect. Because of their local knowledge and influence, turf gangs can be very useful indeed to larger organised crime groups, and many of them are effectively affiliated members of much larger gang organisations.

Territorial gangs are sometimes considered defensive in nature, and so assumed to be less dangerous than other types of street gang, since expansion isn't necessarily a constant goal. This can be a misleading viewpoint. While not characterised by quite the same propensity for violence that other types of gang are known for, they will not hesitate to use extreme violence to defend the areas that they consider theirs. Territorial gangs have the potential to evolve into 'corporate' gangs once they have progressed deeply enough into the illegal drug industry. At the point that drugs production and distribution becomes a primary interest, the gang is often fully absorbed into a larger organisation, losing its identity.

CORPORATE OR ORGANISED GANGS

The second type of gang, referred to as organised or corporate, is the most common face of street-gang America. For them crime is a business. This type of gang is heavily involved in predatory criminal activity, in particular drug trafficking, and is now the focus of most official anti-gang initiatives. Corporate gangs are aggressive, determined, and exhibit a level of casual violence that sets them apart from other types of street gang. Corporate gangs are by nature expansionist, and are constantly seeking to spread their influence by annexing or destroying surrounding groups. Almost all are loosely affiliated with one or more TCO networks. The level of organisation that the corporate gangs exhibits approaches that of some of the international organised crime groups, but constant attrition, gang wars, and the focused action of law enforcement and social programmes tends to disrupt their operations. Many of these gangs are so large that they are considered criminal syndicates in their own right. Through alliances across the nation these syndicates gain power and influence.

The Four Nations are the four most powerful gang alliances operating within the United States today

Formed by vast webs of treaties from numbers of small 'incorporated' gangs, these groups work as independent corporations for self-defence and profit.

The members of the Four Nations divide into two pairs of bitter enemies, thanks to their ongoing rivalries. The Crips and Bloods both originated in Los Angeles at the tail end of the 1960s and the early 1970s, where they came into conflict over control of the drug trade. They have since enjoyed a high media profile, including numerous articles and movies. The other two groups, the Folk Nation and People Nation, are based in Chicago, where they have come into conflict for similar reasons. They remain bitter rivals.

The Crips and the Bloods have expanded to include chapters as far away as Chicago and New York. Operating like organised crime groups, they have the highest profiles of the Four Nations. Having been boosted into prominence by the anti-drug campaigns in the 1980s, this pair of gangs quickly rose into national powers. Both are continuing to engage in the recruitment of new gangs, and their influence expands yearly. The Crips wear blue as their primary colour, and the Bloods have chosen red.

The focus of both organisations remains drug trafficking, something that has brought them into conflict with a number of other groups, both large and small. Offering such groups the opportunity to either join or die, they have steadily gained affiliates and have increased in power and prominence. Although both maintain strong connections to the international drug pipelines, they are largely self-sufficient in supply, end-product synthesis, and management. A number of facilities across the United States are maintained that allow raw materials to be processed into a saleable street product. Their distribution network increases with their growing membership, and they have proven themselves to have the business savvy to manage the growth and new threats.

The worst threat to these gangs has proved to be the conflict between them that began in the late 1970s. Under the coverage of somewhat unwanted national media, they soon became the intense focus of law enforcement. Faced with impending intervention by law enforcement and a determined opponent, both gangs suddenly found themselves vulnerable. After negotiation, a minor truce was declared and each focused their resources on trying to expand their enterprises across the nation faster than the other, in order to gain the upper hand. The relative peace between the groups has been maintained, although occasional flare-ups of violence still occur between incorporated gangs.

The Folk Nation (or just Folks) and People's Nation rival the Crips and Bloods in size. Unlike their West Coast rivals, the two Chicago gangs are better described as alliances. Instead of forcibly adding new gangs to their organisations, they are formed by genuine partnerships of member gangs that still enjoy a high degree of independence. Given the faction mentality of such groups, the amount of co-operation and mutual support exhibited by member gangs has been surprisingly strong. Both groups, unlike the Crips and Bloods, also maintain a strong presence within the nation's prison system, where they dominate. The Folks and People's Nations also take great pride in their Chicago origins.

For street gangs that value their autonomy, the decision to join an alliance such as the Folks or People's Nation isn't taken lightly. To do so means submission of their own interests in favour of a larger group that may contain former enemies. It also means that they have instantly acquired a host of deadly enemies in a number of other previously unknown gangs. For many, the advantages more than balance out, especially for a smaller gang or one that is on the decline. Membership within an alliance creates a support structure that they would never have had access to before. Protection, recruitment assistance, and a solid supply of contraband or other services are automatically within reach. As is true at an individual level with all street gangs, trying to break free of the larger group is strongly discouraged, and usually results in violence.

The People's Nation represents a strong multi-racial alliance of gangs, largely led by a group known as the Latin Kings. The symbols of the People's Nation include a five-pointed star, the number five and a crown, and these are prominently incorporated into many of the member gangs' symbols. Some rivalry between factions of the member groups is known, but it is kept firmly suppressed. Prominent member groups include the Latin Counts, the Vice Lords and the Spanish Lords.

The Folk Nation has taken a highly adversarial stance towards the People's Nation right from its creation. It views the People's Nation as its primary competition. This is reflected in the group's symbols, many of which are corruptions of common People's symbols – such as an upside-down number five or an upside-down five-pointed crown. Member gangs are extremely loyal, and enthusiastically join in this rivalry, which has sparked open conflict on numerous occasions. Other common gang symbols include a pitchfork or a six-pointed star. The most prominent member of this alliance is the Black Gangster Disciples (BGD), which holds a position similar to the Latin Kings. Other groups include the Black Disciples, the Spanish Cobras, and the Two-Sixers.

Relations between the members of the Four Nations have proven interesting to say the least. Recent years have seen increased incidences of peaceful co-operation between the groups in business operations, despite public declarations of hostility. This has been known to occur whenever a significant profit can be reaped, even between the Crips and Bloods, whose members are usually at each other's throats. In most cases, this only happens openly when neither party has the resources necessary to take advantage of the situation, and violence would simply create more problems, perhaps by drawing the attention of other rivals or law enforcement groups. These ceasefires are normally short-lived since not even alliance member groups are able to completely suppress internal friction. While no permanent truce between any of the Four Nations has ever been in place, recent news suggests a disturbing change.

It is not possible to tell if the LA-based gangs are being absorbed or simply joining up, but both the Crips and Bloods have taken on some of the business practices and philosophy of the Chicago-based groups. The ties that are forming seem to be quite strong, which bodes poorly for law enforcement and society in general. Whether future action by law enforcement will be able to exploit the innate weaknesses of the alliances or if a further combination of alliances will occur is unclear at this time. However, as business interests intensify, it seems likely that the Four Nations will follow the lead of the major transnational organisations and put aside their differences – whatever they tell their soldiers on the street.

SCAVENGER GANGS

The third and final gang classification is the scavenger gang. These groups exist for the sole purpose of making money through theft, fraud and deception, rather than drug trafficking and prostitution. By staying away from the drugs trade, they are able to avoid a lot of the violence associated with corporate gangs. Their alternative emphasis leads to quite a difference in attitude and ethos. Non-violent crimes are the norm. Scavengers commonly engage in theft, burglary and robbery. In general, scavenger gangs have better survival rates. They also attract less police attention than corporate gangs, which helps them to prosper.

These gangs also tend to exhibit a degree of specialisation in their choice of target – automobile theft, say, or identity theft – although the level of sophistication and proficiency varies greatly between groups. Scavengers also differ from the other gang types in that they do not tend to claim or defend a set territory. In some cases, they are even nomadic, continually moving to new areas to find new targets and avoid police attention. Their weaknesses lie in the fact that they are loosely organised, tend to have small numbers of members, and do not have the same sorts of useful contacts and connections as corporate as those of territorial street gangs. While their small size and nomadic nature may make it easier to avoid apprehension, their poor organisation leaves them vulnerable to other, more violent groups that may object to their intrusions. Scavenger gangs are generally independent, but TCOs may turn to them when they have need of a particular expertise, such as filling a large order of stolen luxury cars for example, or breaking into a specific computer system.

HATE GANGS

Hate-oriented gangs are unified by arrogance, pride, and a desire to right supposed wrongs or gain vengeance for perceived slights. These groups are made up of individuals who justify their bigotry by painting themselves as the victims of injustice. Facts that might support the bigotry are generally unavailable, but then the members' beliefs don't need any basis in fact. Supposed facts and 'convincing' arguments – a blend of simple lies, invective and quasi-religious dogma – are usually wheeled out to justify actions in the public arena. Even a cursory review of the respective belief systems that these people expound is enough to reveal their statements for what they are – blind, racist propaganda.

A common misconception regarding hate gangs is that their members are poorly educated, unintelligent, or ineffectual. While this may be true in some instances, many of the leaders of these groups are well educated and well read. Unfortunately, even they are unable to objectively review their ideologies and have simply adopted skewed interpretations of facts to support them. Strong beliefs do not allow for any unbiased thought. These groups are dangerous, and should not be underestimated. It is tempting to paint them as bumbling racist fools, but the power of their bigotry gives them a strong tendency towards ruthlessness and the use of violence.

The Ku Klux Klan (KKK) is the most famous of all racist organisations. A white supremacist group, it has its roots in the turmoil of the American Civil War. Known for their use of white hoods and burning crosses, they are infamous for countless assaults, murders, and the harassment of non-whites throughout the southern United States. This group continues to operate and recruit primarily in the south where resentment based in poverty or left over from the Civil War still remains. Although terrorism against non-whites continues, this group has become more subtle in its activities due to the attention of law enforcement and civil rights groups. It now peddles propaganda, hate and smear campaigns, along with drugs and light weapons.

The KKK has strong ties to other white supremacy groups such as the Aryan Nation.

The White Aryan Resistance (WAR) is, as the name implies, a radical white supremacy group. Once labelling itself the 'most vehement racist group in the country', this group has drawn a significant following from likeminded supporters across the nation. It is also known as the first modern hate group to utilise cable access television to spread its ideology, using a programme called *Race and Reason*. Unlike the KKK, the members of WAR are organised as skinhead gangs. This moniker is of course taken from the shaven heads common to many fringe and Neo-nazi groups. The current membership of this organisation is unknown, although it and its associates are still active in a significant number of racist and criminal activities.

The Black Hebrew Israelites (BHI) are extreme black supremacists who claim roots going back to the Civil War era. They claim that Afro-Caribbeans are 'God's true chosen people', while Caucasians are manifestations of incarnate evil, and Jewish people are 'imposters'. In other words, they believe that race war between blacks and whites is inevitable – almost exactly what the KKK and WAR believe, but inverted. While the movement's beginnings were non-violent, hardcore members of the BHI have organised into violent gangs, engaging in physical attacks, murders and general terrorist activities. This is funded by street crime such as assault, drugs trafficking, weapons smuggling and fraud. The BHI maintains a peaceful (if somewhat criminal) community in Israel, but their American sect is considerably more dangerous. Since its leader, Hulon Mitchell Jr (known as 'Yahweh ben Yahweh' – 'God, son of God') was jailed in the 1990s, its power has been considerably diminished.

OUTLAW BIKER GANGS

Although they have been in existence since just after the Second World War, the leather-clad outlaw biker first came into the public eye in 1954, courtesy of Marlon Brando in the movie *The Wild One*. The outlaw biker has become a popular icon for American culture, often promoted as a rebel, a loner or even a disgruntled patriot, but the Hollywood image is as much a romanticised fable as the golden-hearted East End villain. With strong internal structure and business practice, and a whole raft of connections to TCOs, they have become what many believe is the most dangerous drug cartel operating upon US soil. Biker gangs also carry the distinction of being one of the few street gangs to have spread outside national boundaries.

It is important to acknowledge the difference between outlaw bikers and motorcycle enthusiasts. According to the American Motorcycle Association, only about one per cent of motorcycle enthusiasts are part of the criminal element. While many riders may look the part – a Harley-Davidson motorcycle, long hair and beards, leather clothing and a general badass attitude, most aren't involved in the organisations' activities. The image of the tough (and unwashed) leather-clad biker with a noble heart has been used as a smokescreen for years to hide the dangerous villains amongst the harmless rogues. It is an example of a wolf in wolf's clothing, and the rest of the enthusiasts resent it immensely.

The true outlaw biker has many traits in common with other career criminals, including a fondness for shocking violence. Many of them have served considerable stretches of prison time. They also display a complete disregard for the lives of others, callous hostility towards any people outside the organisation and open hatred of law enforcement and government.

Although it is simplistic, the 'us and them' viewpoint is one of the staples of the outlaw biker culture.

Members of bike gangs are strongly loyal to the organisation, to the point of supporting other members in personal and professional matters. Even entire blood-related families are involved, reinforcing gang solidarity and pride. In a sardonic twist, some bikers, especially the Hell's Angels, have started referring to themselves as the 'one-percenters,' referring to the AMA statistic listed above.

By the 1970s, over 900 biker gangs were known to be operating within the USA. Many were small, but some of the larger groups were known to have upwards of 5,000 members. The largest groups remain the Hell's Angels, the Outlaws, the Pagans and the Bandidos. It is estimated that their current total membership reaches well over 200,000.

In the 1980s, law enforcement agencies included biker gangs within their offensive on organised crime for the first time. Existing legislation involving violent crime and the War on Drugs was thought to be sufficient to stop the activity of these groups, but results were uneven at best. Violent and prominent offenders were simply slowed down by incarceration, and the problem of stifling the groups' growth remained. Tougher legislation such as the famous Racketeer-Influenced and Corrupt Organiz-ation (RICO) act gave law enforcement more power. Government agencies including the FBI, the Alcohol, Tobacco and Firearms (ATF) agency, and the Drug Enforcement Agency (DEA) inflicted serious damage. Indictments were lodged against many members, but instead of breaking the outlaw biker gangs, they prodded the gangs into doing the worst possible thing: evolving.

When law enforcement agencies began their assault, gang leaders took many of the steps typical of other emergent crime groups. The gang's organisation was modified to improve strength and security, in some cases along nearly military lines. They were soon ready to take the fight back to the government agencies. The gangs also learned to use the legal system in their favour, using tactics such as disclosure to gain the names and addresses of witnesses, who were killed or intimidated as needed. They also gained valuable information on how law enforcement works, using the information to further hone their operations and even overturn convictions.

Today's biker gangs, like other crime groups that survived law enforcement efforts, have become more organised than before, and they have expanded. American biker gangs have now spread across Canada, Scandinavia, Australia and New Zealand.

Bike gangs are primarily focused towards serving as drugs cartels, but maintain interests in a number of other criminal activities. These include contract murder, intimidation, weapons smuggling and white slavery. The big four groups are all known to engage in all of these activities.

The most famous biker gang are the Hell's Angels, founded in 1957 by Ralph Hubert 'Sonny' Barger Jr. This group is involved in a wide variety of criminal activities, including drug trafficking, prostitution, slavery, vehicle theft, and murder for hire. The gang has two mottoes that sum up their ethos: 'Three people will keep a secret if two are dead' and 'Fuck the world'.

The Outlaws were founded by John Davis in 1959 in Chicago, Illinois and have since grown to about 34 chapters across the US and Canada. Their most lucrative business is drug trafficking, although they also maintain slavery operations and gunrunning rings. Their skull and crossed pistons symbol is taken from the back of

Brando's jacket the in movie *The Wild One*. Their motto is 'God forgives. Outlaws don't'.

Donald Eugene Chambers formed the Bandidos in 1966 in Houston, Texas, and they engage in a variety of illegal activities. These include drug trafficking and production, prostitution, slavery and Mafia-sponsored contract murder. They also have strong connections to the Outlaws, for whom they act as distributors. The symbol and the name for this gang was taken from an advert for Frito corn snacks featuring a character known as the Frito Bandito and their motto reflects the 'one percenter' line – 'We are the people that our parents warned us about.'

The Pagans are the smallest of the big four, with approximately 44 chapters nationwide. They are known for their propensity for violence, and their semi-nomadic nature. The majority of their income comes through drug production and distribution, but they also indulge in mob-sponsored contract murder.

ETHNIC STREET GANGS

Ethnic street gangs first appeared in the United States in the 1830s with the influx of immigrants into New York from Europe. Faced with discrimination, abuse and even overt violence in their new country, members of the newly formed communities were forced to band together for survival. Initially this took the form of self-defence groups and patrols (similar to territorial gangs), but they eventually developed into something far less noble. Taking names such as the Forty Thieves, the Pug Uglies, and the Five Pointers, they began to prey upon the very communities they called home. Although not particularly impressive, they represent the roots of what became the street gangs in the United States today.

Modern ethnic gangs have a great deal in common with the early defence groups of America's immigrant communities, but there are also several important differences. First, the original ethnic gangs were formed as a means of community survival in a hostile society. The modern social landscape, however, has a variety of well-established ethnic communities and is far more accepting of immigrants than the America of the nineteenth century, so self-defence is not a legitimate concern. Secondly, the original ethnic gangs were formed for supposedly noble purposes in the way that territorial gangs sometimes were, but modern gangs do not hold to that. In many cases, the modern groups are formed from the ground up to become corporate street gangs, and immediately start out as predatory in nature. A third difference, and one that is far more disturbing, is that the modern ethnic gang frequently exhibits and maintains advanced connections to organised crime groups in their ethnic homelands. The US gangs are often affiliated with or even extensions of these groups, or in other cases, act as advance scouts for future invasions by their parent groups.

Ethnic street gangs are a separate issue to standard US street gangs, largely due to the strong identity that holds them together. Such groups are bound by common cultural ties, and often held in line by blood ties rather than fear. They also exhibit a high degree of ethnophobia, which is exploited by the group's leaders to maintain a hate-based 'us against them' mentality. This ensures that members and new recruits remain loyal to each other and their superiors to a degree that is not often seen in other gangs. In some cases, personal honour or religion is their primary motivation, making it almost impossible to effectively use traitors, informers or undercover infiltrators.

Ethnic street gangs also tend to base their operations from within a community of people of the same race, as opposed to venturing into mainstream society and taking territory like other gangs. While this may be taken as a further sign of xenophobia or even a lack of familiarity with other cultures, it offers a number of practical advantages that give them the equivalent to a 'home game advantage'. Ethnic gangs, especially those that operate under the authority of organised crime groups, are viewed as authority figures in the community and treated with respect and fear. They have easy access to a strong recruiting base of people who are unfamiliar or afraid of the surrounding culture and can be easily controlled. The language and cultural barriers also provide a formidable defence against the actions of law enforcement agencies. With immigrants being distrustful of outside agencies, few investigating officers are able to find anyone who can or is willing to speak with them. This makes investigations extremely difficult. Given the shortage of American law enforcement officers of certain ethnic origins – particularly Chinese, Japanese and Russian – infiltration of such gangs has proven nearly impossible.

The ethnic gangs operating within the United States today share traits with other street gangs – they are violent, criminally minded, and possess little or no fear of law enforcement. Many of them are well connected to organised crime groups from their origin countries, and often serve as extensions of the parent organisation.

Ethnic Chinese gangs in the US are often associated with a specific meeting place or 'tong'. The meeting place itself may be perfectly legitimate, but it gives the gang a place to socialise. The On Leong gang took its name from the On Leong Merchants' Association, an organisation established in nineteenth-century Chicago to help new Chinese immigrants to acclimatise to America. By operating under the cover of a benevolent organisation and keeping their operations within China-town districts, they were able to avoid the attention of law enforcement for a number of years. This group was heavily involved with gambling, extortion and money laundering, until they came into conflict with an established gang known as the Ping On, sponsored by the Chee Kung Tong. Although the On Leong survived, they were weakened by the war, and currently run a reduced operation.

An offshoot from the All-Mighty Latin King & Queen Charter Nation has operated along the East Coast since the late 1980s. They maintain a strictly Hispanic membership. Like their People's Nation cousins, the All-Mighty Latin King & Queen Charter Nation is building a web of strong connections and alliances with other gangs across the nation. This has helped to spread their influence, frustrating the efforts of law enforcement to dismantle them. Their main profits come from drug trafficking, although they maintain involvement in a wide variety of additional criminal enterprises such as money laundering, gunrunning and extortion. What sets them apart from most other gangs, however, is their brazen attitude towards law enforcement personnel. They are known to issue murder contracts against the police and the FBI liberally, treating officers with the same degree of disdain as they do competitors.

The Local Boys are a Vietnamese street gang based in Chicago that maintains strong connections to Chinese organised crime. They made their appearance in the mid 1990s. Known for their excessively violent activities, they are extremely well equipped and are known to engage in home invasions, contract murder, and extor-tion. For dirtier operations against opponents, the Chinese gangs and tongs often employ them as muscle. When they work on their own behalf, the Local Boys mostly prey upon members of their own community, especially newly arrived immigrants.

The Wah Ching (Chinese People) is known to have an established presence on both coasts of the United States. Once sponsored by the Hop Sing Tong, the street gang dominates the supply of a variety of vices in their areas, including drug trafficking, prostitution and gambling, along with extortion rings and trafficking illegal aliens. They have a reputation for extreme aggression, and at one point their violence was drawing so much attention that the Wo Hop To, a significant transnational Triad, stepped in to tame them.

The Latin Locos are a Hispanic Connecticut-based gang founded in the 1970s, where they controlled the drug trade within a relatively limited area. In recent years, the influence of this group has declined sharply due to a number of factors – the lack of a stable and effective leadership, highly effective action by law enforcement, and strong competition from rival gangs for their territory. The result has been a reduction in membership, both due to attrition and desertion. The Latin Locos are currently considered a 'minor' gang, but their status is in flux and their fortunes may be on the rise again.

Another Hispanic gang known as La Hermandad de Pistoleros Latinos ('Brotherhood of the Latin Gunmen') was apparently formed in Texas in the early 1980s. It is said to have a variety of criminal interests including burglary, assault, gambling rings and drug trafficking. Due to internal friction the Hermandad split into two factions known as the '45s' and the '16/12s', and have expanded greatly from their original power base. They reportedly have been active as far from Texas as New England.

PRISON GANGS

Prison gangs have been around in the USA since the 1960s and 1970s. The War on Drugs of the 1980s saw a huge influx of gang members into the penal system – where they thrived. Imprisonment was viewed with the same contempt that the gangs faced the rest of society, but they had a reason to be cocky. They were entering the penal system in such large numbers that they were able to dominate their new environment. Given their nature of taking advantage of an opportunity, the prisons became the training grounds for the new order. Allegedly, some gang members pursued advanced education while on the inside, so when they got out they were able to help the gangs with state-sponsored degrees in law.

Incarceration also offered the opportunity to forge contacts, many of which had valuable skills to offer. While gang/non-gang status and race issues always coloured contacts in the outside world, the standards are different in prison and new alliances were forged, many of which had the resilience to survive life outside.

Gangs also took advantage of the relative safety and security in prisons, both from law enforcement and other gangs. Incarcerated gang leaders, like Mafia bosses, have proven themselves capable of running their organisations from a cell where law enforcement agents find it difficult to apply pressure. It is also easier to protect leaders in a disciplined environment where groups of well-ordered associates do not draw attention. As a result, the gangs have remained intact, loyal and well structured, and have become a stable part of prison life.

Incarcerated gang members bring the gang identity and mentality with them behind bars. The penal system has attempted to take this into account. As a base rule, gang colours and other markings are not permitted. So gangsters identify themselves by wearing their clothes in a particular way or with verbal codes. Since speech cannot be controlled, passwords and identifier phrases are now the norm.

Current studies show that there are six major gangs recognised as maintaining a significant presence across the entire US penal system. All six are well connected, both to other gangs and to international organised crime.

The largest major US prison gang is a Hispanic group known as Neta, which was initially founded to halt racial violence in Puerto Rico's Rio Pedres prison in the 1970s. The group actively promotes itself as a cultural organisation, and its members are known for their strong stance for an independent Puerto Rico. They have connections to a variety of like-minded radical groups such as Los Macheteros. Some observers say that they enjoy enough political ties to eventually become classed as a terrorist organisation. Neta are a key example of an organisation that takes advantage of the prison environment for recruiting purposes. So far, this has provided the group with a steady supply of new blood, and it is possible that loyal members are inserted specifically into the penal system for this purpose. When operating in prison, this gang has proven to be highly disciplined and well organised. They are the sworn enemies of the Latin Kings and have a high potential for violence.

The second major US prison gang is a white supremacist group known as the Aryan Brotherhood or AB. The AB tends to exercise caution in choosing its fights, but is universally opposed to black gangs and their organisations. They have been known to lend support to individual black factions upon occasion, but this is probably to encourage the disruption of rival gangs. They are particularly hostile towards the Black Guerrilla

Family. The Aryan Brotherhood maintains a working relationship with the Mexican Mafia (La Eme), another prison gang, and connections to other racist groups such as the Dirty White Boys (a faction of the Texas Syndicate), numerous biker gangs, and independent groups. The latter are alternately tolerated or attacked, especially if they attempt to present themselves incorrectly as associates. Symbols for this gang are typical of those chosen by other white supremacy groups, including both Nazi markings (such as the swastika and SS lightning bolts) and Celtic symbols related to Irish heritage.

The Black Guerrilla Family (BGF) was created by George L Jackson, a former Black Panther, while incarcerated in San Quentin prison in 1966. Building upon his philosophy, the BGF has risen to become the most powerful black supremacist group operating within the United States prisons today. Rivalling any of the other five gangs in ferocity and organisation, its influence extends well beyond both the prison walls and national borders. The BGF is the most politically oriented of any of the gangs, even considering Neta and its drive for Puerto Rican independence. This group holds to strong Marxist beliefs, and views the overthrow of the United States government as its primary goal. In many ways, the BGF can be considered a developing terrorist organisation, especially when one considers its earlier connections to the now defunct terrorist groups such as the Weather Underground and the Symbionese Liberation Army.

BGF symbols reflect the gang's philosophy of conflict against oppression and, oddly, against racism itself. Common identifiers include a black dragon attacking a prison tower, or crossed swords with a shotgun. Strong ties are maintained to La Nuestra Familia and a variety of black gangs, including the Black Gangster Disciples and the Crips and Bloods. A mutually hostile relationship exists with the Aryan Brotherhood, the Texas Syndicate and all white supremacist gangs.

The Mexican Mafia (La Eme), as its name indicates, has a primarily Hispanic membership. La Eme was founded in 1957 in the Dual Vocational Center of Los Angeles, a youth offender facility, where it was formed from the core members of a street gang. Since then the gang has gained in strength by maintaining a strong structure and a focused goal. The Eme's core philosophy is that of ethnic solidarity, much like several of the other gangs, but it doesn't differentiate between rivals of any race. Due to its very direct approach against rivals, a 'kill on sight' relationship exists between its members and those of La Nuestra Familia, and it is listed on the Federal Bureau of Prisons' Watch list. La Eme has an active working relationship with the Aryan Brotherhood, a good relationship with the Mexikanemi (with whom they are often confused), and a variety of Latino street gangs. They are known to provide services for organised crime groups, including protection for members of the Italian Mafia.

La Nuestra Familia (NF) originated within Soledad prison in the 1960s as a self-defence group for young Hispanics entering the prison system. Where the Mexican Mafia has its roots in the defence of urban Hispanics, this group is focused upon the welfare of rural Hispanics. Cultural differences between the two's memberships fuelled a bitter hatred that continues today. Conflict between the six gangs is common, but the NF seems to be actively trying to undermine any potential peace with its drive to control all contraband smuggling within the system by any means necessary. This has drawn the attention of prison authorities, but the combined weight of the other five gangs has probably done more to stifle their ambition. Currently, La Nuestra Familia maintains an uneasy alliance with the BGF, although continuing aggression by NF members is proving damaging. They are opposed to the Texas Syndicate and the Aryan Brotherhood.

The Texas Syndicate also began as a defence group for Hispanics within the Texas prison system. The Texas Syndicate believes in ethnic superiority and is actively intent upon proving it. The membership of this group has risen steadily, largely due to their shift on emphasis from solely Texan Hispanics to include Latinos of all nationalities. The Mexican Mafia and La Nuestra Familia remain the primary enemies of the Texas Syndicate. The key reason is most likely competition for resources and manpower, but the NF's push for dominance has certainly not helped. The Aryan Brotherhood is hostile, but a good relationship is maintained with the Black Guerrilla Family.

STREET GANGS AND TCOs

Gangs and organised crime groups have a number of common characteristics, often beginning with similar origins – as groups formed to provide territorial control, ethnic defence, or to monopolise a market. Emphasis upon strong cultural identities, strict codes of conduct, and harsh discipline for disloyalty or failure are also widespread. While street gangs hold a position at the low end of the criminal ladder, they all have the potential to evolve into major players.

The difference between a street gang and a TCOs is in organisation and sophistication. Major TCOs, such as the Mafia, the Triads and the Russian Organizatsiya operate like multinational corporations, with a host of levels of redundancy, smokescreens, and subtle political influences in order to defend themselves from the efforts of international law enforcement – and defeat their rivals. As a result, international organised crime groups have become entrenched in modern society and have proven nearly impossible to destroy.

The street gangs, however, don't enjoy this sort of resilience or level of power. Possessing an often fatalistic world view, gang members accept that they are probably going to die violently. The gangs themselves aren't built for permanence, and a single well-timed strike at the leaders is often enough to annihilate the smaller gangs. Recent movements by gangs to form nationwide alliances have improved their defences against law enforcement, but they still do not possess anything like the power of the TCOs. This lack of ability has been a vital weapon against them in the past, but larger gangs are already learning by example and moving to improve. Their first step is often to build a working relationship with one of the major players.

Working relationships between the two levels are formed because of simple economics and need. Consider drug trafficking as an example. Street gangs are constantly seeking ways to improve their situation, usually by gaining a monopoly on drug trafficking in their locale, but they need to secure a solid supply and gain the force to dominate or destroy their competitors. Such conflicts are usually bloody and provoke costly, long-lasting feuds – such as those between La Nuestra Familia and La Eme, or the Crips and the Bloods. Once a gang has started down this path, there isn't any turning back. Any allies that can be gathered are valuable. It soon becomes about survival.

Meanwhile, organised crime groups are also consistently looking for ways to improve their income, but they bring different strengths with them. They are well financed and well defended, but greed and constant competition pushes them to expand further. Since potential markets such as those offered by the modern United States are ethnically diverse, the groups lack the common cultural and ethnic ties that in the past would have permitted easy penetration. Also, gangs of varying power already control many of these areas, and it can be inefficient and costly to start a war to take it from them. Displacing someone from their home turf is never easy. Instead, the TCOs stay upon the safer path of developing a working relationship with street groups.

The relationships that form between street gangs and organised crime are a delicate balancing act, with each side attempting to take advantage. Normally, the organised crime group takes the dominant role in the partnership, but this can vary depending upon how close the connection is going to be. Limited contract work only requires light involvement so the gang retains a great level of autonomy, but the TCOs need more control if an enduring network is being set up. While there is a big difference for TCOs between using small gangs and larger ones, all are treated with professionally high levels of caution.

Street gangs of all sizes provide TCOs with several important services. Organised crime groups carefully weigh the advantages offered by possible 'partners' against potential threats to find the best candidate. Small gangs without many resources are generally not worth attention, unless they can either be tightly controlled (often through ethnic ties), the gang already has existing ties to the crime group (i.e. the Organizatsiya and its sub-gangs), or the gang can be levered into a manageable alliance. The TCO has to make sure that it remains in a dominant position. By contrast, when dealing with big gangs or alliances of gangs, the TCO's influence is more limited, and negotiations tend to be carried out on an equal basis, but the gang will have more resources, manpower and outlets to offer.

Street gangs have the personnel and infrastructure to operate a distribution network for the products that organised crime supplies, including all kinds of drugs, weapons, and even illegal immigrants. Gangs know their turf intimately, in a way no larger organisation ever can. They have the contacts and resources in a given area to make significantly more profits from it than any outsider could hope to. TCOs have been known to provide street gangs with advice, training, and even additional support when needed.

Enforcement – 'murder for hire' – has been both a profitable business and a vital resource for major criminal operations throughout their history. With increased capabilities of law enforcement to track connections behind crime, the huge pool of expendable assassins provided by street gangs is a valued resource. Gang members provide a deniable way of eliminating opposition, and many long-standing links of this sort exist. The Pagans bike gang, for example, is said to have long worked with the Gamino Mafia family as executioners.

Street gangs also provide an extensive training ground for the criminals of the future. The organised crime groups try to stay aware of the most talented individuals, and may recruit them from the gangs' ranks. Many gang criminals hope to get promoted into the big league, in service to one of the major players.

7. THE FIGHT AGAINST ORGANISED CRIME

EVERYONE'S PROBLEM

The greatest tools to fighting transnational crime are public awareness, understanding and education. Society – from the kids on the street through to directors in the boardroom – needs a good understanding of the real threat posed by organised crime. The TCOs are a lot more than just a topic of conversation and a source of spectacular news stories. The bottom line is that organised criminal activity is not just a source of cheap videos and dodgy hashish. It results directly in job losses and insecurity, low wages, poor working conditions, high insurance premiums, rising street crime, burglary, violence, higher taxation, government instability and weakness, international tension, terrorism, casual murder and even, in some cases, war.

The fight against organised crime needs to take place on three levels – local, national and international. Law enforcement agencies work closely with local neighbourhood groups to stop crime on the doorstep, across agencies within a particular state to keep gangs under control and with agencies worldwide to try to stop international crime. The key to making these initiatives work is simple: co-operation.

LOCAL INITIATIVES

Transnational crime, like many other global phenomena, operates through the trickle-down effect. It manifests on the street in the guise of drug dealers, crack heads, drive-by shooters, muggers, thieves, pimps and prostitutes. Many of these characters might not exist without the presence of a TCO somewhere in the shadows. Any increase in mugging, drug dealing and prostitution in a given area suggests that organised criminals have moved into a neighbourhood.

Any gang that claims a city or section of a city as its territory will have a neighbourhood contact on the ground. In turn, these district agents will recruit other people to work under them, becoming minor bosses in their own right, and using the extra resource of larger affiliation to stamp their authority on the area. These minor bosses will often emulate the activities of their higher-ups, including buying all or part of *bona fide* businesses, in order to gain some legitimacy.

The average police officer can only combat this type of crime on a case-by-case basis. The burden of proof makes it hard to take effective action at street level. Authority is effectively limited to catching a criminal in an act of violence, or stopping a drug dealer with sufficient material on his person to justify prosecution. But an increased number of coppers on the beat and police co-operation with community groups are both somewhat effective ways of preventing crime.

In the UK, the newest initiative in dealing with street-level issues is the revival of the beat patrol. Due to their connection and relationship with the people on their beat, patrolling officers are right on the pulse of the area, and they can identify – or at least make an educated guess at – the general cause of an area's problems. They also give a face and a personality to a person who is often thought of as just a badge, a helmet and a uniform.

Another practice that is proving useful in Britain and the USA is community self-policing. Innovations on this old idea have aided the fight against street level crime, especially where special 'neighbourhood alert' phone lines have been set up. These numbers give the citizenry the power to help bring police attention to specific criminals in their neighbourhoods, but at the same time offer reliable anonymity, preventing reprisals from criminals. In Britain, the national anonymous phoneline Crimestoppers has proved highly effective.

US cities have recently started copying long-standing European plans and many have instituted community policing forums in local areas, where concerned citizens can voice their issues directly to the police and the police can respond. A neighbourhood educated in the methodology and tactics of low-grade criminals is often better equipped to handle threats. If there is a high turnover of street-level punks, and the community takes an active part in suppressing criminal behaviour, the organised criminals will often move on to a more profitable part of town.

Many police departments in Europe and America have also developed ethnically focused crime response units in order to handle criminal activity in their communities. An example is the Los Angeles Sheriff's Department Asian Crimes Task Force. This unit specifically targets the Triad and Yakuza groups and their activities, and makes an effort to recruit ethnically East Asian officers, who are more familiar with the subtleties of criminal activity in LA's Chinatown.

NATIONAL INITIATIVES

To combat the rising wave of gang activity, drug trafficking and organised crime, many national police departments worldwide have formed task forces specifically to target organised crimes. Units of this nature often employ state of the art equipment, and use specially trained officers. For example, the

Royal Canadian Mounted Police (RCMP) have added an organised crime division to its structure, with its own deputy commissioner.

On a state level, the Illinois State Police Gang Tactical Unit in America was founded in 1995. This unit was created to assist police districts in Illinois – the home of two of the Four Nations gangs, the Folks and the Peoples – and also assist federal units in dealing with crime related to gang activity. The unit is specially trained to investigate and deal with high-level gang-related crime. Besides direct action against gangs, the unit also helps communities cope with problems caused by gang crime.

A similar agency is the Italian Direzione Investigativa Anti-Mafia (DIA), or Investigative Anti-Mafia Director-ate, established in 1991. It is made up of collected task forces of officers from the two national Italian police forces, the Polizia Justiciale and the Carabinieri – the Italian equivalent of the US National Guard – along with officers from the Guardia di Finanza (GDF), an agency similar to the Serious Fraud Squad. The DIA reports to the Ministry of the Interior, and it is officially headed up by the General Commanders of the Polizia, the Carabinieri and the GDF, along with the heads of the Italian secret services, Servizio Informazioni Sicurezza Militare – SISMI (military intelligence) and Servizio Informazioni Sicurezza Democratica – SISDE (civil intelligence).

The DIA's sole duty is to investigate organised criminal activity of all kinds, and it has three divisions. First Branch is the analytical division, assessing information and preparing intelligence. Second Branch carries out operations and handles investigations. Third Branch co-ordinates international issues and investigations. In addition to the powers and jurisdictions it holds in its own right, the DIA is entitled to make use of the powers held individually by the Polizia, Carabinieri and GDF.

The DIA has had some notable successes. After a lengthy investigation, the Sicilian Mafia 'boss of bosses' Salvatore Riina was arrested in January 1993. When this was followed in 1996 with the arrest of his heir, Giovanni Brusca – who was said to be responsible for more than one hundred murders, including setting off the bomb that killed Giovanni Falcone, a leading Italian anti-crime prosecutor – the Mafia knew that they were in trouble. In October 2000, Italian authorities captured Salvatore Genovese, one of the most wanted Sicilian Mafia leaders, who had been a fugitive for seven years. Genovese is believed to have been the right-hand man of Sicilian Mafia boss Bernardo Provenzano, who is also a fugitive. Thanks to these recent victories, the Sicilian Mafia has been thrown into disarray – the weakness of the Mafia's hierarchical structure has always been the danger associated with losing top figures. It remains to be seen whether they will rally, or whether other groups will take over its operations.

Investigating organised crime is a dangerous job. High-profile murders of Italian judges are only the tip of the iceberg. Undercover officers and agents have always been critically important to the fight against organised crime but, if they are found out, their lives are worthless. Undercover police working on gangs typically have to infiltrate from the ground up, but criminal organisations are slow to trust any low-ranking member with important information or firm contacts and links. It can take years to penetrate an organisation and then build a case that holds water.

On 20 April 2002, the results of a three-year investigation came to a head with the arrest of 45 mobsters linked with the Genovese family in the USA.

During the course of the investigation, 73 further arrests had taken place, including those of 34 of the family's capos. US federal representatives said that the high levels of infiltration of the family and leveraging of key witnesses were the primary factors influencing the investigation's success. It was described as the most extensive undercover mob operation in a decade.

Getting rid of just one branch of the organisation doesn't always help much in the short term. Once the primary group in an area has been toppled, another will come in and fill the void left at the top. However, the effects are cumulative. Any major loss does hurt a TCO, and can help to throw its operations into some chaos for a while. Areas that become known as dangerous for criminals will be avoided as much as possible in a TCO's international operations – frequent busts are bad for profits. Besides which, no TCO has totally unlimited resources. It is possible to weaken any particular organisation to the point that it cannot compete, as the disintegration of the massive Colombian cartels into many smaller operations clearly shows.

The National Criminal Intelligence Service (NCIS) is the United Kingdom's national agency with the responsibility for obtaining information related to organised criminal activity, and then working with that information. It aims to offer a range of strategic intelligence reports. These include profiles and assessments of major criminals and the groups that they run, and detailed analyses of significant organised criminal activity, particularly as it affects British interests. NCIS also attempts to promote and support co-ordinated responses and collective information sharing at all levels. The agency works both nationally and internationally with a range of law enforcement agencies, governmental bodies and other interest groups and think tanks. Its international interests are represented by UK-focused branches of Interpol, Europol and the Drug Liaison Officer network.

BILATERAL EFFORTS

One response at national level is to set up joint co-operative efforts to combat specific regional issues. These bilateral agreements can help to provide effective limits on the expansion of given criminal organisations by targeting both ends of an operational chain. In time, the agreements can also result in broader regional control efforts, providing greater opportunities for efficient collaboration between agencies.

Bilateral co-operation is a common way of co-ordinating responses, and a prime example of this was the joint US/Hungarian initiative set up late in 1998. Primarily designed to intensify the attack on transnational organised crime and terrorism, this plan targeted already existing criminal groups with the intention of disrupting and dismantling them. The US government offered wide-ranging FBI investigative support to the Hungarian law enforcement bureaux. This took many forms, which included loaning the Hungarians several teams of FBI agents with expertise in organised crime matters, expert laboratory and forensic assistance, criminal justice information systems support and prosecutorial assistance for joint strike forces.

This was not the first time that the two countries had co-operated to work against organised crime. In early 1995, the ILEA (International Law Enforcement Academy) was created and given headquarters in Budapest in recognition of the dual threat that transnational organised crime and terrorism posed for Hungary and the USA. The ILEA has become the principal mechanism for the exchange of information and expertise between the Hungarian National Police and the FBI in areas relating to international organised criminal activity. Modelled after the FBI National Academy in Virginia, and funded by the FBI, the ILEA has trained hundreds of police officers from 20 countries across central and Eastern Europe, and works with law enforcement agencies, government departments and other relevant organisations nationally and internationally.

Several US federal agencies contribute special agents for the academy as instructors. These organisations include the Drug Enforcement Administration, the United States Secret Service, the Bureau of Alcohol, Tobacco and Firearms and the United States Customs Service. ILEA has not only been successful in building professional relationships between individual officers, but it has also led to closer relationships between the participating countries. In many cases, it has helped form a new spirit of co-operation and assistance between different national organisations. For example, introductions to various officials attending the ILEA have led directly to Hungary and Romania incorporating various memorandums of understanding that have provided the foundation for subsequent national treaties. Regional co-operation and information sharing is also facilitated by the FBI-sponsored Central European Working Group, which has 13 member nations, and focuses on the identification of common law enforcement threats and the establishment of lines of communication among partner countries.

The FBI has also initiated bilateral task forces on specific projects with Greece and Italy. The Italian-American Working Group (IAWG) is described as 'one of the most successful international bilateral working groups in addressing common crime and terrorism issues'. Starting off from humble beginnings in the 'Pizza Connection' cases, and the investigations of the assassinations of Judges Giovanni Falcone and Paolo Borsellino, it has developed to the point where it is considered the current benchmark for success of bilateral initiatives within the law enforcement world. The success of the IAWG is attributed to 'developing cop-to-cop partnerships, and focusing upon a common and agreed strategy'.

In early 1998, in the wake of attacks on US diplomatic and military personnel by the Greek terrorist organisation Seventeen November, the FBI entered into partnership with the Greek police. The Seventeen November Task Force began operations in mid 1998, and consisted of two FBI Special Agents and three Greek police officers. With the support of the Hellenic police and access to FBI resources and expertise in the US, this small team made the first ever arrest of a member of the Seventeen November, a group that had been eluding the Greek police for a number of years.

Bilateral organisations are usually formed to combat a common problem. The British and Italian police have joined forces to combat traffic in human beings. Britain is often the final destination for traffickers, and Italy is one of the most common arrival points in Western Europe, because of its proximity to the East, and its long, complicated coastline. The two countries are well placed to intercept criminals engaging in the trade, so co-ordinating their actions to disrupt the routes and apprehend criminals makes good sense.

A list of initiatives for the newly formed bilateral team has been drawn up. Among other things, the UK and Italy plan to lead the creation of an EU-wide immigration liaison officer network in the Western Balkans, increase bilateral exchanges of immigration experts and – following the successes of an Italian-Albanian initiative – to promote the deployment of expert teams from EU member states to the Western Balkans to provide on-the-ground support.

At higher strategic levels, both the UK and Italy intend to work together to encourage the EU Police Chief's Task Force to drive forward operational work against human traffickers, and push for tough EU-wide penalties for human trafficking and transporting illegal immigrants. The crime is currently far less severely punished than drugs smuggling. These goals will be encouraged on a number of different levels, starting with lobbying for fuller use of – and commitment to – Europol. The people working within the agreement will liaise closely on these issues in European Union and G8 discussions. The UK government believes that 're-inforced EU-level action, driven by Italy and the UK, will make a significant impact on the trafficking of people, reducing the horror and suffering it produces.'

INTERNATIONAL CRIME-BUSTING

Like all official programmes that span a number of countries, operations to work against transnational crime groups are extremely complicated, and get bogged down in any amount of red tape – and that's before the criminals start bribing officials to be obstructive. Most of the current measures that are in place to help control the problem are primarily national, or cover a single region at best. Even worse, governmental response varies widely between nations. It makes it very difficult for law enforcement agents to take effective action. The TCOs do not take even the slightest notice of national borders, and make full use of the different remits of their opponents. National and regional efforts are therefore already starting out on the back foot, and the organisations know exactly how to take advantage of the problems they face.

Consequently, a number of genuinely global initiatives have been put in place to do what they can to counteract the problems of regionality. The most significant of these is Interpol, the second largest international organisation in the world after the United Nations. It has 178 members, and is tasked with supporting all groups dedicated to the detection and prevention of organised crime. The organisation has bureaux in every member state, and each of the National Central Bureau (NCB) operations is linked directly to every other, and to the organisation's General Secretariat in France. The NCBs broadcast information about high-profile wanted criminals, missing persons and important thefts, as well as sharing any pertinent information about criminal methods – such as the new Black Cocaine. In addition to pooling information, Interpol also organises a range of conferences and other summits to discuss different areas of current criminal activity, and co-ordinates information on specific topics.

In order to help the organisation respond to the challenges of organised criminal activity, Interpol adopted a new three-year plan in 1998. The aim was to help the organisation increase its scope in order to boost its effectiveness. The aims of the plan were to shift operations to a project-by-project basis for dealing with significant areas of transnational criminal activity, to improve the Secretariat's abilities to analyse and assess data, to set up direct connections to the member states' national police forces, and to improve data security when embarking on joint projects. The Organised Crime division of the General Secretariat was duly renamed the Organised Crime Projects branch (OCP).

Interpol has a wide range of different projects on the go at any one time. Project Millennium was initiated in 1998 to examine the Russian Organizatsiya and other

East European groups, and Project Bridge was started in 1999, to look into ways to collect information about human trafficking. Interpol also runs the IWETS database (the Interpol Weapons and Explosives Tracking System), which is the only international system dedicated to tracking stolen weapons.

Interpol is far from the only transnational law agency, of course. The United Nations maintain a number of initiatives and programmes which, like the European initiatives, are aimed at providing information, and a clear legislative framework. The UN's core anti-TCO programmes are co-ordinated by the Centre for International Crime Prevention (CICP), which acts as a general advisory, clearing house and research data centre for organised criminal activity. Other United Nations groups and initiatives include the Inter-regional Crime and Justice Initiative (UNICRI), the Drug Control Programme (UNDCP), and the UN Convention on Transnational Organised Crime, which provides a set of international protocols and agreements to help strengthen individual government actions. These include the *Protocol to Prevent, Suppress and Punish Trafficking in Persons, Especially Women and Children*; the *Protocol against the Smuggling of Migrants by Land, Sea and Air*; and the *Protocol Against the Illicit Manufacturing of and Trafficking in Firearms, Their Parts and Components and Ammunition*. Other accords of the convention include measures to help strengthen efforts against money laundering, to promote witness protection, global definitions of criminal activities and international co-operation, and to make extradition simpler.

THE EUROPEAN UNION

Within Europe, there are a growing number of regional and sub-regional organisations and initiatives that have been tasked with addressing part or all of the problem of organised crime, corruption and illicit arms trafficking.

Europol is the European Union institution that seeks to improve effectiveness and co-operation between legal authorities in the member states. It is designed to help prevent and combat all international crime, both organised and casual.

The Maastricht Treaty of 1992 first made reference to agreeing the inception of Europol. Based in The Hague in Holland, Europol started limited operations on 3 January 1994, in the form of the Europol Drugs Unit (EDU). Over the following years, other elements of criminal law were added to the protocols, and the Europol Convention was ratified by all Member States and finally came into force on 1 October 1998. Even with all the paperwork finally taken care of and all of its mandates in place, Europol only started to take on its full activities during the summer of 1999.

Europol's remit covers most forms of serious crime. This specifically includes drug trafficking and distribution, illegal immigration networks, vehicle theft and trafficking, trafficking in human beings (with particular reference to slavery and child pornography), forgery of money and other forms of payment, trafficking in radioactive and nuclear substances, money-laundering activities associated with any of the above crimes and, especially, terrorism.

Its mandate applies wherever an organised criminal structure is involved, and two or more member states are affected. Before a second country becomes involved in the criminal activity, it remains a matter for that country to deal with on an internal basis, as it would any other serious domestic crime. If the initial run of co-operation is successful – and so far, it has been – the mandate may be extended in the future to cover other forms of organised crime, such as fraud.

Europol has no executive or operational powers, and no capacity to gather evidence, but it is not supposed to be a European FBI. Rather than having a large physical presence, it maintains a massive intelligence-based capability, and offers a range of information, services and products to operational teams across the EU. Each one of these services is available to all of the member states, and includes a Europol Liaison Officer network. This network facilitates the rapid and secure exchange of intelligence and operational requests between member states, and helps with the provision of analytical support to international investigations. Other resources, in the form of strategic assessment papers that offer specialised expertise in areas of particular interest are also made available to all as soon as they are published.

It should be noted that Europol co-operates closely with the Scheveningen Information System framework, and with Interpol, the European Commission's Anti-Fraud Co-ordination Unit (UCLAF) and the World Customs Organisation (WCO), as well as some third-party countries, primarily those who are candidates for admission to the EU. These organisations have a similar administrative base to Europol itself, and as such are easier for it to deal with than specific governments may prove to be.

The actual powers of Europol are decided by the European Parliament, and are all ratified in agreement with the various member states. An example of this was the Tampere summit of October 1999, which called for the establishment of a European Police Chiefs' Operational Task Force. This was to exchange experience, current best practice and information on current trends in cross-border crime, and to contribute to the planning of operations. Rather than set this task force up independently, it was decided to progress it as a sub-structure with Europol. It generally takes between two and three years to implement new task forces in normal circumstances, but thanks to the Europol framework, the group was set up within six months, and had its first meeting in April 2000.

Over the years, Europol's jurisdiction has increased in scope. In November 2000, the Council asked member states to increase support for joint investigative teams by providing Europol with any detailed knowledge they had of the criminal world. This included – but was not limited to – assisting with co-ordination of operations, providing advice on technical matters, and helping with the analysis of offences. Europol's remit was also extended to include money laundering in general, regardless of the type of offence from which the laundered proceeds originated. This was passed by a European Council act of 30 November 2000, and was hailed as a breakthrough by most of the states.

The criminal organisations are profit-making companies, and their main interest is money. This has led to a number of operations and initiatives designed to help fight money laundering, which remains the primary means by which the TCOs are able to realise profits. The European Union battle against money laundering has become harder since the borders between western and Eastern Europe have been opened. The difficulties lie not so much in a lack of co-operation, but rather in the manner in which this co-operation is organised. The Commission's money laundering directive, 308/91 – which has been accepted by most of the EU – contains eight sections aimed at helping to deal with money laundering at an individual bank level. These include provisions on each individual bank's duty to identify customers and transactions. Professional practices on the part of bank workers and internal controls for bank security are the most important parts of the provisos contained in the directive. Under the terms of the directive, all transactions over 15,000 euros need to be certified, and similar rules are also to be applied to non-financial activities. However, of the countries within the agreement, only Italy, Germany, Belgium, Ireland, Netherlands and the UK have introduced laws that criminalise all money laundering of illegal profits. These particular laws specifically include all profits generated from drug trafficking, terrorism, arms trafficking, prostitution, smuggling, extortion, organised crime and other illegal activities. These activities are illegal in all of the member states, but some of the countries have yet to rule that criminal proceeds from these activities can be confiscated.

One major issue for crime fighters in the EU has been the creation of a border-free zone known as Scheveningenland. Formed early in 1995, Scheveningenland is an area of free circulation within the European Union created by the original seven signatories to the Scheveningen Agreement – Belgium, the Netherlands, Luxembourg, France, Germany, Portugal and Spain. The purpose of the agreement is to allow the free flow of goods between the nations in question. The terms of the agreement were later incorporated into the EU framework generally in the Amsterdam Treaty of 1997. Britain was one of the few members to opt out. The agreement has both helped and hindered the fight against TCOs.

But in order to maintain internal security, a variety of 'behind-the-border' measures were taken by the majority of EU states under the terms of the Scheveningen Agreement. These include reinforcing external borders, harmonising visa policies, setting criteria that will indicate a country responsible for processing an asylum request, putting in place procedures for co-operation between police forces, agreeing a common policy on legal aid in criminal matters, having a common extradition treaty, and taking specific steps to combat drug trafficking and control firearms and munitions use.

Additionally, the Scheveningen states have developed the Scheveningen Information System (SIS), which provides police and immigration officials across the region with a multinational database of criminal suspects, stolen vehicles and forged money. Within each country, an NSIS (National Scheveningen Information System) network is linked to the Central Scheveningen Information System (CSIS) installed in Strasbourg. This system can be accessed by any of the member states, and can transfer information at a massively enhanced rate. To help facilitate the co-operation between member states, and to step up the war on international drug trafficking, the Scheveningen countries have also all sent liaison officers to each other's embassies. This is considered both a privilege and a benefit for those countries that participate.

Critics have argued that open borders invite increased trafficking of drugs, people and arms, and can lead to an increase in illegal immigration and bogus asylum claimants. The problem is not so much the internal borders within Scheveningenland – as the whole point is to do without them – but rather the external controls that each of the border countries has to take care of. A 1998 report on cross-border surveillance by an organisation called Statewatch notes that 'the relevant provisions of the Scheveningen Convention do not fully correspond to the tactical requirements of the police'. What the report means by this is not that the Scheveningen Agreement is not viable, but that while in theory the ideas presented are perfectly sound, in practice, they are often too difficult or expensive to properly maintain. Certainly, smuggling becomes a lot cheaper when you only have to get over one border.

The police in many of the Scheveningen states have expressed a growing number of concerns. The primary cause of police concern in this matter involves missing rights of arrest for pursuing officers in some states. In theory, the Scheveningen Agreement guarantees that officers who need to pursue criminals across borders will be guaranteed full help apprehending the fugitives in question. In practice, this is often hampered by the fact that politicians in each country want the credit for the capture of the criminals, and so the proposed spirit of equity often falls by the wayside in the pursuit of brownie points. The situation is not helped by the problem of poor judicial record keeping in some of the member states.

Some EU member states have opted out of Scheveningen – or like the UK, have proposed limited participation – because of a reluctance to abandon passport controls on internal movements within Scheveningenland. In the UK, which has far more problems than most with illegal immigration, Scheveningenland is seen by many politicians as a way of giving up the last line of defence in exchange for what seem to be dubious benefits.

The EU has also taken specific measures to combat organised crime – and address worries about criminal gangs in former Soviet bloc countries that wish to join the EU in the future. On 25 May 1998, Ministers of Justice of EU member states and the applicant countries within central and Eastern Europe signed the EU Pre-Accession Pact on Organised Crime. The pact promises to intensify existing police, customs and judicial co-operation between the EU and its would-be members in order to strengthen measures against international organised crime within the applicant states before they are admitted to the Union. The pact contains a list of international instruments dedicated to facilitating police, customs and judicial interaction that will serve as a basis for co-operation. The pact's emphasis particularly lies in the exchange of information between enforcement departments in order to smooth along investigations, as well as to help when longer-term strategies are put in place.

A group of experts from the signatory countries to the pact has been given responsibility for its implementation. The list of the tasks associated with the pact centre around identifying and counteracting threats connected to transnational organised crime. Tasks also include monitoring and evaluating various actions taken to counteract crime in each of the participant countries. Organisers also plan, execute and then evaluate specific projects. In the course of its duties, the pact's trustees are expected to be in regular contact with Europol. By implementing the accords of the pact, applicant countries try to ensure that their standards of law enforcement are tight enough to avoid posing an internal threat if they are made full members of the European Union.

Another strategy involving applicant countries is the Central European Initiative (CEI). This is a loose grouping of 17 countries whose main objectives are to contribute to the economic development of central Europe. To this end, they are involved in a number of programmes and initiatives to promote that goal. These include strengthening stabilisation within the region, promoting European integration, and supporting those CEI member countries that are not yet part of the EU in their progress towards integration. The basic structural component of the CEI is the working group. To date, 18 CEI working groups have been instituted, including one that focuses on combating organised crime. Establishment of an information network on organised crime strengthened co-operation and judicial actions across CEI member states. The CEI Bratislava Centre for Combating Drug Trafficking was also formed hand-in-hand with the information network.

At a conference held in Trieste in March 2001, CEI Ministers of Justice approved a declaration on judicial co-operation among member states. The declaration called for harmonisation of legal systems, improved legal assistance and judicial co-operation between CEI members. By making the CEI countries more united in their approach to crime, the members hoped to bolster their efforts against the criminals. The declaration also called for the establishment of joint investigative bodies in relation to specific crimes. The ministers also agreed to work out ways in which they could facilitate the exchange of liaison magistrates. Finally, they also sought the enlargement of the CEI Working Group on Combating Organised Crime, so as to encompass matters related to the improvement of judicial co-operation and mutual legal assistance.

THE FUTURE

By their very nature, the new wave of transnational criminal organisations poses a challenge that cannot easily be answered by traditional methods. Law enforcement agencies have to come up with new responses that are innovative in both content and execution. Single-nation initiatives are insufficient – transnational criminal activities may cross any number of borders, and involve witnesses, evidence and procedures across a whole number of different jurisdictions. Naturally, this causes a number of severe problems. National interests, political point scoring, differences in criminal systems and varied loopholes across the world mean that there is little hope of seeing a law enforcement agency that has the same scope and power as the immense organisations it is trying to fight. While governments remain disorganised and unco-operative, the major TCOs will continue to run rings around them.

In a recent development, the public has started showing increasing signs of unhappiness with current government practice in dealing with organised crime. Six of the men involved in the killing of Giovanni Falcone were released as part of a bargain under which they turned state's evidence over to the magistrates. This produced a very negative reaction amongst the Italian public and even some Italian legislators. There was a lot of criticism about the nature of agreements offered to convicted criminals in exchange for testimony. In many cases involving similar treatment of informers, the public often come away from the whole matter with a strong sense of betrayal. This is particularly true for the victims of any crimes committed by the criminal involved in the agreement. Unfortunately, such deals have to be made in order to ensure the co-operation of convicted criminals in cases of this nature. It is easy to see this sort of deal as a defeat, but it is more accurate to think of it as a compromise that will eventually lead to more criminals being taken down.

However, the alternative to proper judicial process – a strong police state that does not worry about the burden of proof – can be just as horrifying as any criminal activity. Rio de Janeiro, the capital of Brazil, is a city of more than 11 million people. It has been suffering from endemic levels of street crime and violence related to drugs and TCO activity. Police there are confiscating more than ten thousand firearms a year, and barely making a dent. The city itself has half a million legally registered firearms, and it is thought to hold millions more illegal ones. Brazil in general – and Rio in particular – have been criticised by many countries for their poor record of human rights in regard to the excessive violence used by their police in dealing with criminals. In 1994, more than 1,400 children were killed in the vast shanty towns that dot the city. The police were responsible for many of these killings, stating that many of the children were committing much of the rampant crime in the city.

According to the *International Crime Threat Assessment* report, the expansion of transnational criminal organisations could possibly come from several sectors. As a specific instance, a radical breakdown of the Communist system in China could very easily intensify the power and influence of Chinese criminal organisations in much the same way that the Bulgarian groups managed to capitalise on the fall of the Soviet Union. This could then provide the Chinese groups with a safe-haven for expanding criminal operations abroad.

More generally, there are several opportunities for further expansion. Large transnational criminal syndicates are becoming more self-sufficient as they gain better access to highly trained individuals. They are becoming able to produce or acquire, move, market, and distribute drugs and other contraband without any reliance on outside criminal brokers or crime groups. Criminal groups are also taking advantage of new advances in scientific and manufacturing technique to produce new synthetic drugs and better, higher-quality counterfeit products. These include a range of hi-tech components that can find their way into commercial transportation or military programmes. Also, as the world continues to computerise, groups can gain significant advances in their earning power by taking on small groups of talented hackers. With muscle and corruption to back them up, good hacking teams can get into just about any computer system there is. Hi-tech crime is already an important growth sector, and it could have a significant impact.

Criminal organisations with access to extensive weapons arsenals might be able to use that leverage to gain a far more significant role in brokering illicit arms transactions for foreign armies, militias, or insurgencies. It is not impossible to think that they might be able to displace the brokers and businesses that dominate the current grey arms market. If they were able to do so, the TCOs could quite feasibly develop easy access to significant mercenary armies in their own right. Most worryingly of all, though, there is a possibility that dedicated criminal states might start to arise – countries that not only tolerate transnational crime groups, but that actually make a point of actively supporting them in return for a share of the profits.

There are no easy answers. National efforts are too weak to make any headway, while local politics and nationalist sentiments hamstring international ones. However, this does not change the one simple fact that if the world's governments do not do *something* soon to curb transnational crime, the situation is going to get worse for all of us. A lot worse.

Look out for other compelling, all-new True Crime titles from Virgin Books

MY BLOODY VALENTINE – Couples Whose Sick Crimes Shocked the World

Edited by Patrick Blackden

Good-looking Canadian couple Paul Bernardo and Karla Homolka looked the epitome of young, wholesome success. No one could have guessed that they drugged, raped and murdered young women to satisfy Bernardo's deviant lusts. Nothing inspires more horror and fascination than couples possessed of a single impulse – to kill for thrills. Obsessed by and sucked into their own sick and private madness, their attraction is always fatal, their actions always desperate. The book covers a variety of notorious killer couples: from desperados Starkweather and Fugate, on whom the film *Natural Born Killers* was based, right through to Fred and Rose West, who committed unspeakable horrors in their semi-detached house in Gloucester, England. With contributions from a variety of leading true crime journalists, *My Bloody Valentine* covers both the world-famous cases and also lesser-known but equally horrifying crimes.

£7.99 ISBN: 0-7535-0647-5

DEATH CULTS – Murder, Mayhem and Mind Control

Edited by Jack Sargeant

Throughout history thousands of people have joined cults and even committed acts of atrocity in the belief they would attain power and everlasting life. From Charles Manson's 'family' of the late 1960s to the horrific Ten Commandments of God killings in Uganda in March 2000, deluded and brainwashed followers of cults and their charismatic megalomaniac leaders have been responsible for history's most shocking and bizarre killings. Jack Sargeant has compiled twelve essays featuring cults about whom very little has previously been written, such as the Russian castration sect and the bizarre Japanese Aum doomsday cult that leaked sarin gas into Tokyo's subways.

£7.99 ISBN: 0-7535-0644-0

DANGER DOWN UNDER – The Dark Side of the Australian Dream

Patrick Blackden

Australia is one of the most popular long-haul tourist destinations, but its image of a carefree, 'no worries' culture set in a landscape of stunning natural beauty tells only one side of the story. *Danger Down Under* lets you know what the tourist board won't – the dark side of the Australian dream. With a landscape that can be extremely hostile to those unfamiliar to its size and extremes, and an undying macho culture – not to mention the occasional psychotic who murders backpackers, or crazed gangs of bikers and cultists – there is much to be cautious of when venturing down under.

£7.99 ISBN 0-7535-0649-1

November 2002

TEENAGE RAMPAGE – The Worldwide Youth Crime Explosion

Antonio Mendoza

Columbine High School, Colorado, spring 1999. Twelve of its schoolchildren and one teacher lay dead. Two boys have gone on a killing spree, venting their anger at their classmates before turning their guns on themselves. Cases such as Columbine are occurring with increasing regularity – and guns are not always involved. In Japan in 1998, a 13-year-old schoolboy murdered his teacher in a frenzied knife attack. What is happening in society that young people are running amok, fuelled by hatred and nihilism, with little regard for their own lives and the lives of those around them? Expert crime writer Antonio Mendoza investigates this worldwide problem and comes up with some shocking findings that call for a global rethink on how we bring up – and punish – those responsible for the worldwide teenage crimewave.

£7.99 ISBN: 0-7535-0715-3

December 2002

FEMALE TERROR – Scary Women, Modern Crimes

Ann Magma

Statistics show that female crime and female violence is on the rise, particularly in America where, in 1999, over two million violent female offenders were recorded and the rise was cited as 137%. Women are becoming an ever-growing presence in crime statistics, and a major force in both organised crime and terrorism. In the last ten years they have also come to the fore as homicidal leaders of religious sects and gun-toting leaders of Los Angeles street gangs, whose members are every bit as tough and violent as their male 'gangsta' counterparts. From Ulrike Meinhof to Wafa Idris; from IRA terrorists to Mafia godmothers, this book will look at the rise and rise of female terror.

£7.99 ISBN: 0-7535-0718-8

January 2003

MONSTERS OF DEATH ROW – Dead Men and Women Walking

Christopher Berry-Dee and Tony Brown

From the cells of Death Row come the chilling, true-life accounts of the most heinous, cruel and depraved killers of modern times. At the time of writing, there are 3,702 inmates on Death Row across the USA, many of who have caused their victims to consciously suffer agonising physical pain and tortuous mental anguish before death. These are not normal human beings. They have carried out serial murder, mass-murder, spree killing, necrophilia, and dismemberment of bodies – both dead and alive. In these pages are to be found fiends who have stabbed, hacked, set fire to, and even filleted their victims. So meet the 'dead men and women walking' in the most terrifying true crime read ever.

£7.99 ISBN 0-7535-0722-6

The best in true crime from Virgin Books

How to order by mail:

Tick the box for the title/s you wish to order and complete the form overleaf. Please do not forget to include your address. Please check month of publication of later titles.

From Cradle to Grave	Joyce Eggington	0 86369 646 5	☐
Perfect Victim	C. McGuire & C. Norton	0 352 32561 5	☐
Precious Victims	Don Weber & Charles Bosworth	0 86369 598 1	☐
The Serial Killers	Colin Wilson & Donald Seaman	0 86369 615 5	☐
The Last Victim	Jason Moss	0 7535 0398 0	☐
Killers on the Loose	Antonio Mendoza	0 7535 0681 5	☐
Crossing to Kill	Simon Whitechapel	0 7535 0686 6	☐
Lone Wolf	Pan Pantziarka	0 7535 0617 3	☐
I'll Be Watching You	Richard Gallagher	0 7535 0696 3	☐
Unsolved Murders	Russell Gould	0 7535 0632 7	☐
My Bloody Valentine	Ed. Patrick Blackden	0 7535 0647 5	☐
Death Cults	Ed. Jack Sargeant	0 7535 0644 0	☐
Danger Down Under	Patrick Blackden	0 7535 0649 1	☐
Teenage Rampage	Antonio Mendoza	0 7535 0715 3	☐
Female Terror	Ann Magma	0 7535 0718 8	☐
Monsters of Death Row	Christopher Berry-Dee & Tony Brown	0 7535 0722 6	☐

Please send me the books I have ticked above.

Please enclose a cheque or postal order, made payable to Virgin Books Ltd, to the value of the books you have ordered plus postage and packing costs as follows:

UK and BFPO – £1.00 for the first book, 50p for each subsequent book.

Overseas (including Republic of Ireland) – £2.00 for the first book, £1.00 for each subsequent book.

If you would prefer to pay by VISA, ACCESS/MASTERCARD, DINERS CLUB, AMEX or SWITCH,

Please write your card number and expiry date here

Card no.

Expiry date:

Signature

Send to: Cash Sales, Virgin Books, Thames Wharf Studios, Rainville Road, London, W6 9HA

Please allow 28 days for delivery.

Name

Address

Post Code